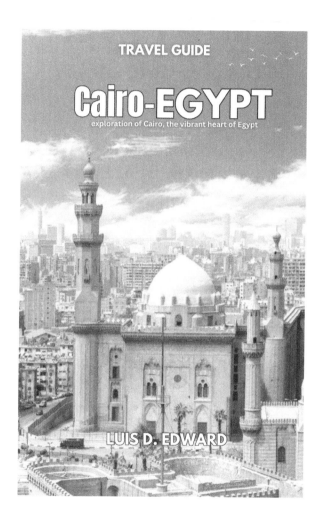

TRAVEL GUIDE

Cairo-EGYPT

exploration of Cairo, the vibrant heart of Egypt

LUIS D. EDWARD

Cairo Egypt
Travel Guide 2024

**exploration of Cairo,
the vibrant heart of Egypt**

Luis D Edward

Table of Contents

Chapter 3: Modern Cairo 110

Chapter 4: Adventures in Cairo 134

Greetings from the enchanting city of

Cairo, Egypt!

Welcome, and thank you for choosing Cairo, a city known for its rich history, captivating landscapes, and vibrant cultural tapestry. Get ready to immerse yourself in the awe-inspiring beauty of ancient wonders, savor the delicious local cuisine, and embark on a plethora of thrilling adventures as you explore this extraordinary destination.

Upon your arrival in Cairo, you'll be immediately captivated by the city's unique charm. The grandeur of iconic landmarks and the bustling energy of its streets set the stage for an unforgettable travel experience. Cairo, with its timeless history and modern vibrancy, offers a myriad of opportunities to discover ancient wonders, delve into diverse cultural experiences, and create lasting memories.

As you venture into the heart of Cairo, don't miss exploring the historical gems that define this remarkable city. From the awe-inspiring Pyramids of Giza to the cultural richness of Islamic Cairo and Coptic Cairo, each corner tells a tale of Egypt's enduring legacy.

Cairo is not only a treasure trove of history but also a vibrant hub of contemporary life. Discover architectural marvels in New Cairo, stroll along the Nile Corniche, and indulge in the city's diverse nightlife and culinary delights. From traditional Egyptian dishes to international gastronomic experiences, Cairo's culinary scene promises a feast for your taste buds.

For the adventurous souls, Cairo offers a plethora of outdoor activities. Take a felucca ride on the timeless Nile, embark on camel and horseback tours, and explore the desert surrounding this dynamic city. Day trips to nearby wonders and scenic flights over the captivating landscapes are also on the agenda for those seeking extraordinary adventures.

Cairo's nights come alive with a mesmerizing display of starlit skies and the sounds of the city. Whether you're gathered around an evening campfire, stargazing at captivating events, or embarking on night excursions to witness nocturnal wonders, Cairo's nightscape offers a truly magical experience.

Whether you're traveling solo, with family, or friends, Cairo extends a warm welcome to all. Explore the city's diverse attractions, create timeless memories, and revel in the harmonious blend of ancient wonders and modern vitality that defines Cairo, Egypt. Get ready to embark on a journey of a lifetime in this spectacular destination. Marhaban!

Cairo's Historical Mosaic

Cairo, Egypt's beating heart, presents a multifaceted mosaic of history that spans thousands of years. The city's legacy is intimately intertwined with its diverse inhabitants, who have shaped its destiny through countless generations. Since ancient times, Cairo has been a center of civilization, home to Pharaohs, and later a crossroads for various cultures and empires, from the Romans and Byzantines to the Arabs and Ottomans.

The city's historical journey is marked by its enduring monuments, the most iconic being the Pyramids of Giza, standing as testament to the ingenuity of ancient Egyptians. Cairo's evolution continued through various eras, each contributing unique chapters to its story. Islamic Cairo, a UNESCO World Heritage site, reflects the city's medieval Islamic history, with its intricate mosques, madrasas, and architectural wonders.

The arrival of European influence in the 19th century introduced new dynamics to Cairo's landscape. The city began to embrace modernity while maintaining its rich cultural heritage, evident in its architecture, art, and urban planning. The British occupation played a pivotal role in shaping modern Cairo, contributing to its cosmopolitan character.

In the 20th century, Cairo emerged as a cultural and political hub of the Arab world, with landmarks like the Egyptian Museum and Cairo Tower adding to its allure. The city has also been a center for intellectual and artistic movements, influencing the broader region and beyond.

Today, Cairo stands as a bustling metropolis that celebrates its ancient roots while looking towards the future. The city is a living museum, where the legacy of pharaohs coexists with vibrant contemporary life. Its citizens continue to preserve their rich traditions and cultural identity, creating a harmonious blend of the old and the new.

As you navigate through the streets of Cairo, take time to absorb the historical layers that make up the city's unique character. From the footsteps of ancient rulers to the modern-day pulse of its busy streets, Cairo offers an immersive journey through time. Discover, learn, and immerse yourself in the captivating charm of this eternal city, where history is not just remembered but vividly alive.

Cairo's Population and Cultural Tapestry

Cairo, the vibrant capital of Egypt, is not only famous for its historical landmarks but also for its diverse and dynamic populace. Let's explore the fascinating fabric of Cairo's people and culture.

Population: Cairo's population, estimated at over 9 million, creates a bustling and multicultural metropolis. The city is a melting pot of people from across Egypt and the world, contributing to its dynamic cultural blend. Among the many communities present are Egyptians of various backgrounds, along with expatriates and immigrants, enriching Cairo's diversity.

Cultural Diversity: Cairo's culture is a captivating amalgamation of its ancient heritage and the influences of its diverse residents. Here are some key aspects of Cairo's cultural mosaic:

Ancient Egyptian Heritage: The legacy of ancient Egypt adds a profound layer to Cairo's cultural landscape. From the Pharaonic monuments to the influence on language, religion, and customs, this ancient heritage continues to be a source of pride and identity.

Islamic and Coptic Christian Traditions: Cairo is known for its Islamic architecture and is home to the historic Coptic Christian community. The city's mosques, churches, and synagogues reflect the religious diversity and tolerance that has been a part of its history.

Arts and Expression: Cairo is a hub for Egyptian and Arab art and culture. From traditional crafts like carpet weaving and pottery to contemporary art, music, and cinema, the city is a center of creative expression.

Culinary Fusion: Cairo's culinary scene is a blend of local and international flavors. Egyptian cuisine, with its use of fresh, locally sourced ingredients, is influenced by Mediterranean, Middle Eastern, and African cooking traditions. The city offers everything from traditional Egyptian street food to global cuisine.

Urban Lifestyle: Cairo's urban lifestyle is a mix of tradition and modernity. The city's bustling streets, markets, and public squares are hubs of daily activity and social interaction. Modern developments coexist with historic neighborhoods, showcasing the city's evolving identity.

Heritage Preservation and Modernity: Cairo actively works to preserve its rich heritage while embracing modern development. Efforts to restore historic buildings and districts go hand in hand with urban development projects, reflecting a balance between conserving history and modern progress.

As you explore Cairo, immerse yourself in the vibrant colors of its streets, the rhythmic sounds of its bustling markets, and the rich tapestry of its cultural traditions. Cairo's diverse culture adds a unique depth to the experience, leaving lasting memories for those who explore this magnificent tapestry of life.

Cairo, Egypt's weather

Cairo, the expansive capital of Egypt, has a distinct climate that greatly influences the way of life and activities in the city. Cairo experiences scorching summers and mild winters, making it a hot desert climate in contrast to the tropical Maasai Mara, Kenya. Here's a detailed look at the weather trends in Cairo:

Warm Summer Months (May through October):

High temperatures are typical throughout this time, with maxima frequently reaching 35°C (95°F) or more in the hottest months, such as July and August.

There is essentially little rainfall during these months, and the climate is typically dry.

Though they are not as cold as they are in the winter, nights can still be a welcome break from the heat of the day.

The warm weather makes it perfect for visiting Cairo's indoor attractions, such as museums, or for leisurely activities that take place later in the evening when it's cooler.

Season of mild winter (November to April):

Cairo's winters are renowned for their mild and comfortable temperatures.

This season's temperatures, which range from 10°C (50°F) to 20°C (68°F), make it pleasant for sightseeing and outdoor exploration.

There is not as much rain as there is in the summer, but it does fall more frequently, albeit in lighter showers.

Because of the ideal weather for touring historical buildings and outdoor markets, this season is very popular with travellers.

The seasons of transition (spring and autumn):

The months of September and October (fall) and March and April (spring) mark the change from summer to winter's scorching temperatures.

The weather is usually pleasant and moderate during these months, while sandstorms, or "Khamsin" as they are called locally, can occasionally occur in the spring.

These times of year are ideal for exploring outdoor sites and taking in Cairo's lively street life due to the temperate climate.

Features of the General Climate:

Cairo has an arid environment with long, scorching summers and short, mild winters due to its location in the northeastern region of the Sahara desert.

The microclimate of the city is significantly influenced by its vicinity to the Nile River, especially in the sections nearer the riverbank.

Effects of Climate Change Worldwide:

Cairo's climate is changing as a result of global climate change, just like that of many other cities throughout the world. This could mean more intense temperatures and erratic weather patterns.

Cairo's climate, with its distinct hot and mild seasons, is an essential part of the city's attractiveness and allure and has a big impact on both the daily lives of its citizens and visitors.

Cairo, Egypt's Religious Diversity

Cairo has a rich religious tapestry that is intricately woven into its historical past, unlike Maasai Mara, Kenya. The city is renowned for its wide range of religious practices, which are a reflection of centuries' worth of historical and cultural influences. An outline of Cairo's religious variety is provided below:

Islam: Cairo is a major hub of Islamic culture, with a large number of venerable mosques and other establishments. With a predominance of Sunni Muslims, the majority of the population is Muslim. Minarets dot the skyline of the city, and the cadence of the call to prayer reverberates through the busy streets. For the people of Cairo, Islamic customs and traditions are an integral part of their everyday existence.

Coptic Christianity: With a substantial Christian population, Cairo is a major hub for Coptic Christianity. Ancient Coptic churches, including as the famous Hanging Church and the Coptic Museum, can be found in the city. Copts add to the rich religious tapestry of the city by celebrating their religious customs and ceremonies.

Judaism: Cairo has a long history with Judaism, even if the city's Jewish population has declined over time. The Ben Ezra Synagogue, which was built in the ninth century, is a significant example of Cairo's Jewish history. Even though it's a tiny community now, Cairo recognises its historical contribution to religious tolerance.

Other Christian denominations: Catholicism and Protestantism are two of the other Christian denominations practiced in Cairo, in addition to Coptic Christianity. These populations live side by side with the predominantly Islamic and Coptic influences, adding to the religious heterogeneity of the city.

Religious Syncretism: Cairo demonstrates some degree of religious syncretism, much as Maasai Mara. A distinct cultural and religious identity has been fostered in the city by the mingling of various religious aspects. There are several facets of everyday life, holidays, and religious rituals where this syncretism is apparent.

Sufism: Within Islam, Cairo is the epicentre of Sufi mysticism. The religious environment of the city gains a spiritual and mystical dimension from Sufi orders and their rituals. Sufi rituals, such as dhikr (remembrance of God), are performed in a variety of locations and offer a singular spiritual experience.

Interfaith conversations: Interfaith conversations are a common way to highlight Cairo's religious variety. Diverse religious groups live together, promoting harmony and understanding between them. The goal of events, conversations, and projects is to encourage interfaith harmony and tolerance.

the coexistence of Islam, Coptic Christianity, and remnants of Judaism characterise Cairo's religious environment and contribute to the city's distinct historical and cultural identity. Cairo's varied religious traditions have shaped the city's rich history and way of life, becoming an integral part of Cairo's fabric.

Cairo, Egypt: A Captivating Vacation Spot

Cairo, which is in the centre of Egypt, is becoming a popular tourist destination due to its exceptional combination of historical grandeur, vibrant urban life, and rich cultural diversity. Cairo, well-known for its historic sites, lively marketplaces, and the mythical Nile River, offers a journey that will never be forgotten. Here are some reasons to visit this historic city:

Investigating the Past:

The Sphinx and Giza Great Pyramids: Admire these historic marvels of the world, which bear witness to Egypt's magnificent architecture and rich past.

Numerous Historic Sites Explore a plethora of other historic locations, such as the Egyptian Museum, which has a sizable collection of artefacts, and the Saqqara Necropolis.

Beautiful Cityscapes:

Views of the Nile River: The Nile, the lifeblood of Egypt, is ideal for a leisurely felucca ride and provides stunning views. Explore the Old Cairo neighborhood's winding streets and stop at notable Islamic and Coptic sites, including the well-known Khan El Khalili bazaar.

Egyptian Traditions:

Cultural Immersion: Savour the distinct cuisine, music, and artwork of Cairo. Explore authentic coffee shops to experience the friendly hospitality of Egypt.

Cultural Festivals & Events: Take part in customs and celebrations that highlight Cairo's rich cultural diversity.

Contemporary Attractions:

Tower Views: Offering sweeping views of the city, the Cairo Tower contrasts historic buildings with the contemporary urban environment.

Bright Nightlife: Cairo's vibrant nightlife, which offers a wide range of entertainment opportunities, reflects the city's modern side.

Observing Birds in the Nile Valley:

Rich Avifauna: A variety of bird species can be found in the Nile Valley and surrounding areas, providing birdwatchers with a great experience.

Preservation of Cultural Heritage and Conservation:

Preservation Efforts: Cairo promotes sustainable tourism to safeguard its priceless landmarks and is actively committed in the restoration of its historical heritage.

Various Choices for Accommodation:

Luxurious Hotels to Boutique Stays: Cairo has a variety of lodging choices, including charming boutique stays in old neighbourhoods and opulent hotels with views of the Nile.

Combining Pleasure with Adventure:

During the day, explore lively marketplaces, museums, and historic ruins.

Calm Evenings: Savour Egyptian cuisine at a nearby restaurant or take a peaceful Nile boat in the evenings.

Cairo provides a singular vacation experience by fusing the energy of contemporary city life with breathtaking historical heritage. Cairo is a place that offers an adventure unlike any other, leaving tourists with enduring impressions of Egypt's ancient splendour and modern appeal. Its iconic landmarks are combined with its rich cultural history.

Cairo, Egypt: Cultural Tapestry Unveiled

Nestled within the vibrant heart of Egypt, Cairo is not just a city; it's a dynamic cultural tapestry that weaves together ancient history, modern influences, and a rich heritage. Here are some key facets that distinguish the cultural landscape of Cairo:

Historical Enclaves:

Giza Pyramids and Sphinx: Behold the awe-inspiring wonders of ancient Egypt, including the iconic Pyramids of Giza and the Sphinx, narrating tales of pharaohs and timeless architecture.

Historical Districts: Explore the enchanting streets of Old Cairo, where Coptic and Islamic landmarks stand testament to centuries of cultural amalgamation.

Cultural Immersion:

Local Markets and Cafés: Immerse yourself in the bustling life of Cairo by strolling through vibrant markets like Khan El Khalili and savoring traditional coffeehouse experiences.

Festivals and Events: Engage with the city's cultural vibrancy through various festivals and events, celebrating art, music, and local traditions.

Modern Perspectives:

Cairo Tower Views: Gain a panoramic perspective of the cityscape from Cairo Tower, offering a juxtaposition of historic charm against modern urban development.

Contemporary Nightlife: Experience the modern side of Cairo through its lively nightlife, showcasing a blend of traditional and modern entertainment.

River Nile Serenity:

Nile River Cruises: Revel in the tranquility of the Nile River with a cruise, witnessing Cairo's skyline against the backdrop of this legendary waterway.

Religious Diversity:

Religious Landmarks: Visit prominent religious sites such as the Hanging Church, Ibn Tulun Mosque, and the Sultan Hassan Mosque, reflecting Cairo's religious diversity.

Syncretic Practices: Witness the syncretism of various religious influences, where ancient traditions harmonize with the teachings of Christianity and Islam.

Architectural Marvels:

Historical Structures: Admire Cairo's architectural brilliance through structures like the Saladin Citadel and the historic Al-Muizz Street, where medieval charm meets contemporary life.

Museums and Art Galleries:

Egyptian Museum: Explore the treasures of the Egyptian Museum, housing artifacts that span the millennia of Egyptian civilization.

Contemporary Art Spaces: Delve into Cairo's thriving art scene with visits to contemporary galleries, showcasing a fusion of traditional and modern art.

Local Cuisine and Culinary Scenes:

Traditional Egyptian Dishes: Indulge in Cairo's culinary delights, from local street food to exquisite traditional dishes, reflecting the city's diverse gastronomic heritage.

Dining Experiences: Enjoy a mix of outdoor dining in bustling markets and elegant experiences in restaurants that blend modernity with tradition.

Cairo invites visitors to uncover its cultural layers, where ancient wonders coexist with the vibrancy of contemporary life. This unique blend creates an enchanting experience, leaving travelers with enduring memories of Cairo's cultural richness and its harmonious embrace of history and modernity.

Getting to Cairo Egypt

There are a number of options available when visiting Cairo, Egypt, according to your interests and location. Cairo, a significant centre of culture and history in the Middle East and North Africa, has excellent international connections, mostly via Cairo International Airport, which serves as the city's main entry point.

Flight Options to Cairo: The primary airport for travellers entering Egypt is Cairo International Airport (CAI). Being one of Africa's busiest airports, it provides a plethora of international connections.

Originating in Europe:

Major European cities like London, Paris, Frankfurt, and Rome provide direct flights.
Regular flights are offered to Cairo by airlines like EgyptAir, British Airways, Lufthansa, and Air France.
Originating in North America:

Although they are less frequent, direct flights are still offered from places like Toronto and New York.

Airlines with connecting routes include EgyptAir, Delta, and Air Canada.

From the Middle East:

several direct flights from major cities such as Beirut, Riyadh, and Dubai.

Frequent services are offered by airlines such as EgyptAir, Saudi Arabian Airlines, and Emirates.

Originating in Asia:

Connection flights are available from major cities such as Beijing, Tokyo, and Mumbai.

Airlines with layovers in their respective hub cities include Emirates, Qatar Airways, and Etihad Airways.

Originating in Africa:

flights from key African cities, such as Addis Ababa, Nairobi, and Johannesburg, both direct and connected.

Services are offered by Ethiopian Airlines, EgyptAir, and other African airlines.

From New Zealand and Australia:

Usually, flights connect at hubs in Asia or the Middle East.

For these routes, Qantas, Emirates, and Singapore Airlines are frequently utilised.

Alternative Travel Routes:

By Water:

Alexandria and other Mediterranean ports can provide access to Cairo, which can then be reached by car or train.

By Land:

Although it is conceivable, overland travel from nearby nations is less popular because of the larger distances and variable travel conditions.

Considerations for Visitors to Cairo

Verify whether you require a visa in order to enter Egypt. A lot of tourists can apply online for an e-Visa or obtain a visa upon arrival.

Flight Time: This varies a lot based on where you depart and whether you have any layovers.

Health and Safety: Remain informed about any travel warnings and any vaccinations or other health requirements.

Egyptian Pound is the local currency (EGP). Major credit cards are widely accepted, however it's still good to have some local money.

Cultural Awareness: It's critical to comprehend regional traditions and attire expectations in order to have a polite visit.

Cairo offers a fascinating blend of modern and historical elements, and travelling there is not too difficult from most places in the world. Cairo offers a distinctive and unforgettable experience, whether you're touring the lively marketplaces, seeing the famous pyramids, or conducting business there.

Accommodation Option

There are numerous lodging alternatives in Cairo, Egypt, to suit a variety of tastes and price ranges. Travellers can choose from a variety of accommodations in the city, ranging from opulent hotels to affordable hostels, to make their stay comfortable. An overview of the different kinds of lodging in Cairo is provided below:

1. Luxury Hotels: First-Class Hospitality: Cairo is home to a number of five-star establishments with opulent features such magnificent rooms, fine dining restaurants, and spas.

Well-known Chains: Four Seasons, Kempinski, and Marriott are just a few of the brands with properties in desirable locations, many of which feature views of the Pyramids or the Nile.

Boutique Luxury: Some hotels offer a more distinctive experience by fusing local charm with luxury amenities.

2. Mid-Range Hotels: Cosy and Inexpensive: These lodging options include standard amenities like Wi-Fi, air conditioning, and on-site food.

Chain and Independent Options: These include both global chains and neighbourhood motels that provide a good mix between affordability and comfort.

3. Low-Cost Hotels and Hostels: Economical Places to Stay: Perfect for travellers on a tight budget, these lodging options provide standard amenities at a reduced cost.

Shared Facilities: Hostels frequently offer communal areas for sleeping and using the lavatory, which makes it easy to meet other visitors.

4. Apartment Rentals: Comfortable Setting: If you're looking for a more homely atmosphere or longer stays, renting an apartment or a studio is a terrific choice.

Different Platforms: Listings ranging from contemporary flats to more conventional homes may be found all across Cairo thanks to services like Airbnb.

5. Guesthouses and B&Bs: Personalised Experience: These places offer a warm, welcoming ambiance and frequently serve breakfast.

Cultural Immersion: A more genuine taste of Egyptian hospitality can be had by staying in a bed and breakfast.

6. Boutique and Themed Hotels: Special Themes: These lodging options offer a distinctive cultural experience, frequently revolving around Egyptian art or history.

Charming and Intimate: They are usually smaller and provide a more individualised experience.

Considerations for Selecting a Place to Stay:

Location: If possible, try to stay close to popular sights or in places with good public transport connections.

Amenities: Consider what features, like Wi-Fi, air conditioning, or a restaurant on the premises, are essential to you.

Reviews: To determine the calibre of the lodging, read through prior visitors' web reviews.

Cost: Cairo has options for all budgets, though costs might differ significantly depending on amenities and location.

Cultural Experience: Certain lodging options, especially boutique hotels or guesthouses, can provide a more in-depth look at the local way of life.

Advice for Making Hotel Reservations in Cairo:

To ensure the greatest prices and availability, make reservations well in advance, especially during the busiest travel seasons (October to April).

Think About Proximity to Attractions: If you have certain places you want to visit, staying close by can help cut down on travel time.

Safety: Although travelling to Cairo is typically safe, it is nevertheless preferable to stay in respectable lodgings in well-known neighbourhoods.

transit Access: Take into account how simple it is to use public transit, as well as the availability of ride-sharing services and taxis.

There are lodging alternatives in Cairo for every kind of visitor, matching the diversity of the city. Cairo's hospitality will undoubtedly improve your stay in this energetic city, whether you're searching for opulence on the Nile, an affordable hostel in the centre of town, or a charming guesthouse in a more sedate area.

Top Attraction

Egypt's vast capital, Cairo, is a city rich in culture, history, and breathtaking architecture. For any traveller, it is a veritable gold mine of attractions. While in Cairo, take into account the following must-see sights:

1. The Sphinx and the Pyramids of Giza: Iconic Landmarks: These famous buildings, the last standing wonders of antiquity, are a must-see.

The Great Sphinx is a magnificent and enigmatic figure that watches over the Giza plateau.

2. The Egyptian Museum: Antiquities: Contains a vast array of antiquated Egyptian relics, including Tutankhamun's treasures.

Explore Egypt's rich historical legacy, spanning from prehistoric periods to the Greco-Roman era.

The lively Khan El Khalili Bazaar, which dates back to the 14th century, is a bustling marketplace that sells a variety of goods, including jewellery, spices, and traditional crafts.

Cultural Experience: An exciting location to buy for trinkets and get a taste of the native way of life.

4. Islamic Cairo: Historical Area: A section of Cairo characterised by mosques, madrasas, and other Islamic-style buildings.

Al-Azhar Mosque: One of the oldest mosques in Cairo and a well-known hub of Islamic scholarship.

5. Coptic Cairo: Christian Heritage: Discover the historical landmarks and ancient churches that trace the origins of Christianity in Egypt.

The Hanging Church is a well-known church with exquisite furnishings and a distinctive high location.

6. The Citadel of Saladin: An impressive Islamic structure from the Middle Ages that provides sweeping views over Cairo.

Mohamed Ali Mosque: Often referred to as the Alabaster Mosque, this Egyptian Ottoman-style mosque is a masterpiece.

7. The Nile River: This famous river is a great place to take a classic felucca ride; it's especially lovely after dusk.

River Cruises: Dinner cruises provide a distinctive perspective of the city together with cuisine and entertainment.

8. Cairo Tower: Panoramic Views: This location is excellent for taking pictures of cityscapes and offers a bird's-eye perspective of Cairo and the Nile.

9. Saqqara and Dahshur: Ancient Necropolises: Home to the Red and Bent Pyramids, as well as the Step Pyramid of Djoser, which provide insight into the early stages of pyramid construction.

10. Modern Cairo: Modern Attractions: Take a look around contemporary neighbourhoods like Zamalek, which is well-known for its cafes, galleries, and gardens.

Organising Your Trip:

Timing: To avoid crowds and the noon heat, try visiting key attractions early in the morning.

Guided Tours: Guided tours can offer important context and perspectives for historical locations.

Dress Appropriately: It is advised to wear modest apparel, especially when visiting places of worship.

Transportation: Make appropriate travel plans because Cairo traffic can be quite congested. Metro, taxis, and ride-hailing apps are all viable choices.

Advice: Drink plenty of water, particularly in the summer months.

Cultural Sensitivity: Show consideration for regional traditions and customs.

Cairo is a safe city overall, but you should always be mindful of your surroundings and possessions, particularly in crowded areas.

Cairo is a remarkable tourist destination because of its attractions, which combine dynamic modern life with ancient history. Cairo guarantees an amazing experience whether you're visiting the historical treasures, perusing the extensive museum collections, or taking in the local way of life in the markets and cafes.

Cultural Experience

Egypt's Cairo is a historical and culturally rich city that provides a wealth of experiences for those wishing to learn more about its past. You should think about the following cultural activities when you visit Cairo:

1. Traditional Egyptian Cuisine: Regional Flavours: Savour traditional Egyptian fare such ful medames, falafel, and koshari.

Street Food: For a fully immersive food experience, visit your neighborhood's markets and street vendors.

2. Tea and Shisha in a Café: Café Culture: Enjoy a tea and a hookah (shisha) in a traditional Egyptian café throughout the evening.

Socialising: Cafés serve as gathering places for conversation, people-watching, and socialising in addition to serving drinks.

3. Traditional Music and Dancing Shows: Cultural Events: Take in a traditional music and dance display featuring Egyptian heritage.

Experience the captivating Sufi dance known as Tanoura, which consists of whirling skirts.

4. skill and Calligraphy Workshops: Arabic Calligraphy: Master the skill of Arabic calligraphy, which is highly regarded in Islamic culture.

Visit nearby art galleries to see both traditional and contemporary Egyptian artwork.

5. Local Markets & Bazaars: Visit Cairo's most well-known market, Khan El Khalili, which is renowned for its lively ambiance and wide selection of merchandise.

Buying souvenirs: Stock up on spices, handicrafts, and mementos.

6. Coptic Cairo Pilgrimage: Religious Heritage: See historic Coptic churches, such as the Church of St. Sergius and Bacchus and the Hanging Church.

Spiritual Experience: Take in the religious customs of Egypt's Christian community by attending a Coptic church.

7. Exploring Islamic Cairo: Al-Azhar Park: Unwind in this exquisitely designed park located in the centre of Islamic Cairo.

Historical Mosques: Take a tour of historically significant mosques like the Ibn Tulun and Sultan Hassan mosques.

8. Workshops on Traditional skills: Take part in workshops to learn about traditional skills like glassblowing, carpet weaving, and ceramics.

Meet local artists: Engage with talented craftspeople who are conserving Egypt's traditional handicrafts.

9. Dinner and a Nile River Cruise: Take in the lit city skyline while dining on a dinner cruise on the Nile.

Entertainment: Throughout the voyage, a lot of cruises feature traditional music and dance performances.

10. Attend a Local Wedding: Cultural Celebrations: If the chance comes, learning about Egyptian wedding customs can be gained by attending a local wedding.

Enjoy the festive atmosphere filled with dancing, music, and celebrations.

Advice for Experiencing Cultures:

Respect Local Customs: Pay attention to and observe local traditions, particularly when visiting places of worship.

Learn Some Basic Arabic Phrases: Being able to communicate with people in Arabic will improve your relations with them.

Wear modestly: This is especially important while going to places of worship or cultural events.

Engage Locals: Start a discussion with people in the area to learn more about their culture.

Cairo's cultural activities offer a unique and immersive trip into the heart of Egypt's colourful legacy by fusing ancient traditions with modern living.

Culinary Delights

In addition to its rich historical heritage,

The vibrant Egyptian capital of Cairo is a veritable culinary gumbo. The city's culinary culture is a reflection of its rich cultural background, presenting a myriad of exquisite dishes that are a must-try for every food connoisseur. Here's a tour to some of the gastronomic marvels that Cairo has to offer:

1. Traditional Egyptian Dishes: Koshari: A beloved street snack, koshari mixes lentils, rice, pasta, and chickpeas, topped with a spicy tomato sauce and fried onions.

Ful Medames: A typical breakfast dish made with fava beans, olive oil, lemon juice, and garlic, often eaten with bread.

Molokhia: A classic soup-like meal prepared with minced jute leaves, usually served with rice or bread and chicken or rabbit.

2. Grilled Delicacies: Kebabs and Kofta: Grilled meats, often lamb or beef, seasoned with a range of Middle Eastern spices.

Shawarma: Thinly sliced meat, typically chicken or beef, cooked on a slowly-turning vertical rotisserie.

3. Seafood Specialties: Sayadiyah: A delectable fish dish cooked with rice and a particular blend of spices and caramelized onions.

Fresh Fish from the Mediterranean and Red Sea: Often grilled or fried, and served with traditional Egyptian side dishes.

4. Egyptian Street Food: Ta'ameya: The Egyptian variant of falafel, made mostly from fava beans and laden with herbs and spices.

Hawawshi: Spiced ground meat cooked inside a pocket of pita bread.

5. Sweets and Desserts:

Baklava: A sweet pastry composed of layers of filo, filled with chopped nuts and sweetened with syrup or honey.

Basbousa: A typical semolina cake, often steeped in syrup and garnished with almonds or coconut.

Kunafa: A popular delicacy made of thin noodle-like pastry, or a fine semolina dough, soaked in sweet, sugar-based syrup.

6. Breads and Pastries: Baladi Bread: A traditional Egyptian flatbread, often cooked in a wood-fired oven.

Feteer Meshaltet: A flaky, layered pastry that can be sweet or savory.

7. Beverages: Egyptian Tea: Often served sweet and strong, occasionally with mint.

Qahwa (Coffee): Typically strong and served in small cups.

Fresh Juice Stalls: Widely accessible, offering everything from mango to sugarcane juice.

8. Local Markets and Food Tours: Spice Markets: Explore colourful markets like Khan El Khalili for spices and herbs.

Food Tours: Consider joining a guided food tour to discover Cairo's culinary scene.

Tips for Enjoying Cairo's Culinary Scene:

Street Food Safety: While street food is a must-try, choose busy stalls ensuring fresh and hot meals.

Hydration: Drink bottled water to stay hydrated in Cairo's scorching environment.

Dining Etiquette: It's usual to eat with your right hand when eating traditional cuisine.

Explore Local Eateries: Go beyond tourist places to get real and excellent meals.

Cairo's gastronomic delights are as diverse and rich as its history, giving a voyage of flavors that tell the tale of the city's past and present. Whether you're a fan of hearty street food, elegant seafood, or sweet sweets, Cairo's food scene has something to fascinate every palate.

Introduction

1.1 Welcome to Cairo: The Vibrant Heart of Egypt

Welcome to Cairo, a city that pulsates with the rich fabric of Egypt's history, culture, and current dynamism. As the pulsing centre of this historic land, Cairo invites you to immerse yourself in its intriguing blend of heritage and innovation. Here, amid the renowned landmarks and bustling streets, you'll embark on a journey that spans time, uncovering the riches of Egypt's capital city.

Key Highlights:

Historical Marvels: A Tapestry of Ages

Cairo is home to the awe-inspiring Giza Pyramids, the final surviving wonder of the ancient world. Marvel at the Sphinx standing guard and delve into the mysteries of these architectural wonders.

Explore the historic Citadel of Saladin, a citadel with a commanding outlook of the city, holding mosques, museums, and centuries of history.

Cultural Crossroads: Where Past Meets Present

Wander through the Khan El Khalili bazaar, a labyrinthine marketplace where the brilliant hues of spices, textiles, and trinkets call. Engage with local artists and discover the bustling ambiance of this ancient market hub.

Uncover the riches of the Egyptian Museum, home to a large collection of antiquities, including the golden mask of Tutankhamun.

Islamic and Coptic Heritage: Spiritual Journeys

Visit the old Islamic Cairo area, where tiny passageways lead to great mosques covered with complex decorations.

Explore the Coptic Quarter, discovering historic churches such as the Hanging Church and the Church of St. Sergius and Bacchus.

Nile River: Lifeline of Cairo

Take a leisurely sail along the Nile River, experiencing Cairo's cityscape embellished with modern skyscrapers set against the timeless backdrop of old landmarks.

Enjoy a sunset felucca ride, experiencing the serenity of the Nile as the city transforms with the changing hues of the evening sky.

Modern Elegance: Contemporary Cairo

Experience the vitality of modern Cairo in places like Zamalek and Garden City, with posh boutiques, fashionable cafes, and art galleries.

Ascend to the Cairo Tower for panoramic views of the metropolis, as the Nile delicately winds its way through the urban landscape.

Culinary Odyssey: Tantalizing Tastes

Indulge in a gourmet trip with Cairo's unique cuisine scene. From street food delights to elegant dining, experience the flavors of classic Egyptian cuisine.

Sample aromatic street-side coffees and teas, engaging in the city's social fibre while savouring the warmth of Egyptian hospitality.

Entertainment Extravaganza: Nightlife and Performances

Experience Cairo's dynamic nightlife, where traditional music merges with current beats in colourful places.

Attend a spellbinding performance by the Whirling Dervishes or watch a spectacular music and light extravaganza at the Giza Pyramids.

Welcome to Cairo, where every corner offers a tale, and every stride echoes with the footsteps of pharaohs and the pulse of a lively, modern city. Let the enchantment of Cairo unfold before you, beckoning you to become a part of its intriguing narrative.

1.3 Navigating the City: What to Expect

Navigating Cairo, a frenetic metropolis overflowing with over 20 million people, is an adventure in itself. This section gives crucial information and recommendations to help you travel the city with confidence, ensuring a memorable and pleasant visit.

Getting Around: Modes of Transportation

Taxis and Ride-Sharing Services: Taxis are common and reasonably affordable. For greater convenience and safety, try using ride-sharing applications like Uber or Careem, which offer trustworthy and trackable services.

Public Transportation: Cairo's public transport system includes buses and the metro. The metro is a rapid, economical, and effective way to commute, covering key portions of the city.

Private Car Hire: For extra luxury and freedom, you might opt for a private car hire with a driver. This can be especially handy for exploring sites outside central Cairo.

Walking: In some regions, especially in historic or shopping districts like Khan El Khalili, walking is the ideal way to soak in the local vibe. Be aware of vehicles and tight, congested streets.

Traffic and Navigation Tips

Traffic Congestion: Cairo is infamous for its high traffic, especially during peak hours. Allow extra time for travel, particularly when heading to key appointments or catching flights.

Local Driving Style: Be prepared for a driving style that could seem chaotic. Horn honking is ubiquitous and often used as a communication tool.

Navigation Apps: Utilize navigation apps like Google Maps for real-time traffic updates and directions.

Local Customs and Etiquette

Dress Code: While Cairo is more liberal than some other parts of Egypt, it's advisable to dress modestly, especially when visiting religious places.

Language: Arabic is the official language. English is generally spoken in tourist locations, however learning a few basic Arabic phrases might enhance your experience.

Tipping (Baksheesh): Tipping is prevalent in Egypt. Small tips for services like bag carrying or guidance can be anticipated.

Cultural Sensitivities

Religious Respect: Be respectful to Islamic practices. During Ramadan, eating, drinking, or smoking in public during daytime hours is frowned upon.

Photography: Always ask for permission before taking images of people. Be mindful of photography limitations at certain historic places.

Safety and Health

Safety Precautions: Cairo is typically safe for tourists, but it's wise to stay cautious of your surroundings and keep valuables secure.

Water and Food: It's advised to drink bottled water. Be cautious with street food, and seek busier stalls where food is likely fresher.

Healthcare Facilities: Cairo has good private hospitals and clinics, however it's essential to obtain travel insurance that covers health crises.

Navigating Cairo is a vital element of the journey. Embrace the city's rhythm, remain flexible, and you'll find yourself moving about the city like a local, exploring the various layers that make Cairo an eternally intriguing destination.

Chapter 1

Historical Highlights

2.1 The Pyramids of Giza: Egypt's Eternal Wonders

Welcome to the renowned Pyramids of Giza, a tribute to the ancient Egyptian civilization's architectural brilliance and a must-visit destination on your Cairo adventure. Here's a thorough guide to help you solve the mysteries underlying these colossal constructions.

Historical Marvels:

Pyramid Complex Overview: The Giza Plateau is home to three primary pyramids - the Great Pyramid of Khufu, the Pyramid of Khafre, and the Pyramid of Menkaure. These monuments, erected around 4,500 years ago, served as tombs for pharaohs.

The Great Pyramid of Khufu (Cheops): Standing tall as the tallest and oldest of the three, the Great Pyramid is an engineering wonder. Originally 146.6 meters high, it's constructed of almost 2 million limestone blocks.

The Pyramid of Khafre: Adjacent to the Great Pyramid, it seems taller due to its elevated location and maintains some casing stones at its top. The Sphinx, a gigantic limestone monument with a lion's body and human head, defends the Pyramid of Khafre.

The Pyramid of Menkaure: The smallest of the three, dedicated to Pharaoh Menkaure, it stands at 65 meters and is joined by three smaller pyramids for queens.

Visiting Tips:

Guided Tours: Consider hiring a professional guide to improve your experience with historical insights and lesser-known information about the pyramids.

Visit Timing: The pyramids are open year-round. Morning trips bring cooler temperatures and less crowds. Sunset provides a lovely glow over the structures.

Inside the Pyramids: While access inside the Great Pyramid requires an additional ticket, touring the inner chambers provides a view into the burial chambers and architecture. The Pyramid of Khafre permits admission into the burial chamber for a closer glimpse of the sarcophagus.

Sphinx Viewing: Take time to gaze at the Sphinx, delicately sculpted from a single limestone outcrop.

Capturing the Moment:

Photography Tips: The pyramids give wonderful photo opportunities. Early morning and late afternoon sunlight intensify the structures' golden tint.

Panoramic Views: Climb to higher locations on the plateau for panoramic views of the pyramids against the Cairo metropolis.

Cultural Significance:

Historical Context: Dive into the rich history of ancient Egypt, investigating the purpose and significance of pyramid construction, tied to religious beliefs and the afterlife.

Sound and Light performances: Consider witnessing the captivating sound and light performances conducted in the nights, where the pyramids come to life with dramatic storytelling.

The Pyramids of Giza endure as timeless icons of human achievement. As you stand in their presence, you're not simply witnessing architectural magnificence but connecting with a civilization that influenced the course of history. Enjoy your tour of these eternal wonders.

2.2 The Sphinx: Guarding Ancient Mysteries

The Great Sphinx of Giza, an awe-inspiring ancient edifice, sits as a sentry to the Pyramids and the mysteries of the ancient Egyptian culture. As you visit this huge monument, here's what you should know to fully appreciate its majesty and historical significance.

Enigmatic Structure:

Description: The Sphinx, with the body of a lion and the head of a human, is believed to depict Pharaoh Khafre, linking it to his neighbouring pyramid. Carved from a single slab of limestone, it measures 73 metres long, 19 metres wide, and 20 metres high.

Age and Origin: Dating back to the Old Kingdom, about 2500 BC, the Sphinx is one of the world's oldest and largest statues. The precise motivations for its development and the identity of the modeled face are matters of discussion among historians.

Restoration and Conservation:

Historical Restoration Efforts: Over millennia, the Sphinx has experienced erosion, natural deterioration, and human meddling. Restoration attempts stretch back to the Pharaohs, including major preservation work in the 20th and 21st centuries.

Current Condition: The Sphinx has undergone extensive restoration to maintain its structure and avoid further erosion, notably around the neck and shoulders.

Visiting Experience:

finest Viewing Times: Visit during early morning or late afternoon for the finest lighting and picture options, and to escape the midday heat.

Photography Tips: Capture the Sphinx against the backdrop of the Pyramids for a classic photo. Various angles around the plateau give various perspectives.

Guided Tours: A qualified guide can provide insights into the Sphinx's history, stories, and restoration initiatives.

Cultural and Historical Significance:

Symbolism: The Sphinx symbolizes power and wisdom. Its position, facing the east, indicates a role in guarding the Giza Plateau.

Mythology and Interpretation: Explore the complex tapestry of myths, including tales of the 'Riddle of the Sphinx' and its place in Greek and Egyptian mythology.

Archaeological investigations: The Sphinx continues to be a subject of archaeological investigations and discussions, revealing insights into ancient Egyptian engineering, religious beliefs, and artistic conventions.

Surrounding Attractions:

neighbouring Temples: Visit the neighbouring Temple of the Sphinx, associated with Pharaoh Khafre, providing extra background to the Sphinx's involvement in ancient Egyptian ceremonies.

Sound and Light display: The nighttime sound and light display at the Sphinx and Pyramids gives a spectacular and instructive experience, illuminating the structures in bright colors.

The Great Sphinx of Giza, with its mystery aura and historical significance, delivers a memorable experience. As you stand before this ancient guardian, you are connecting with a culture that has influenced the world for millennia. Enjoy your time learning the secrets and legends of this beautiful monument.

2.3 Islamic Cairo: A Journey Through Time

Embark on a mesmerising tour through Islamic Cairo, a district that unfolds like a living history book, maintaining the splendors of Islamic architecture, culture, and tradition. Let's delve into the ageless appeal of this mediaeval area.

Historical Tapestry:

Architectural Marvels: Islamic Cairo features a treasure trove of architectural marvels, including mosques, palaces, and mausoleums, each narrating tales of bygone ages. Notable structures include the Mosque of Ibn Tulun, Sultan Hassan Mosque, and the Citadel of Saladin.

Medieval Alleyways: Wander through the maze alleyways, where each step echoes the footsteps of mediaeval scholars, traders, and monarchs. The district's layout keeps the essence of medieval planning.

Cultural Landmarks:

Khan El Khalili Bazaar: Immerse yourself in the vivid tapestry of Egyptian trade at Khan El Khalili. This lively bazaar, with its small passageways, is a hotspot for traditional crafts, spices, jewelry, and vivid street life.

Al-Azhar University: Discover the intellectual heart of Islamic Cairo at Al-Azhar, one of the oldest continually operating universities in the world. Its mediaeval mosque and university have been hubs of Islamic learning for over a millennium.

Religious Heritage:

Historic Mosques: Visit the different mosques that stand as architectural marvels, embellished with elaborate decorations and calligraphy. The Ibn Tulun Mosque, dating back to the 9th century, is particularly notable for its unusual minaret.

Religious Tolerance: Islamic Cairo is a witness to religious harmony. Explore the historic Coptic Cairo district nearby, where churches and synagogues stand in harmony alongside Islamic structures.

Preserving Traditions:

Traditional Crafts: Witness craftsmen practicing time-honored crafts, such as delicate woodwork, brassware, and handwoven textiles. Many shops continue to apply skills passed down through generations.

Street cafés and Teahouses: Take a leisurely break at one of the attractive street cafés or teahouses. Here, you can sip traditional Egyptian tea, smoke delicious shisha, and absorb the colourful environment.

Events and Festivals:

Islamic Cultural Events: Check for cultural events and festivals that promote Islamic art, music, and literature. These activities typically provide a better insight into the rich cultural legacy of the district.

Religious events: If your visit matches with religious events, you may observe spectacular processions and festivities around the mosques.

Local Insights:

Guided Tours: Consider a guided tour to acquire in-depth insights into the history and significance of each location. Knowledgeable guides can disclose hidden stories and details.

Respectful Attire: When visiting religious sites, dress modestly out of respect for local customs and religious activities.

Islamic Cairo invites you to stroll through the hallways of antiquity, where every edifice whispers tales of a beautiful past. As you tour this living witness to Egypt's Islamic legacy, you'll find yourself transported to a bygone era of intellectual enlightenment, architectural magnificence, and vigorous cultural interaction.

2.4 Coptic Cairo: Exploring Egypt's Christian Heritage

Embark on a mesmerising tour through the spiritual and historical richness of Coptic Cairo, where Egypt's Christian past emerges in ancient churches, monasteries, and sacred sites. Let's delve into the rich tapestry of this beautiful region.

Historical and Religious Marvels:

Hanging Church (Saint Virgin Mary's Coptic Orthodox Church): Delight in the grace of the Hanging Church, a marvel of Coptic architecture draped over the Water Gate of the Roman stronghold. Admire its gorgeous iconostasis and ancient relics.

Saint Sergius and Bacchus Church (Abu Serga): Step into one of the oldest Coptic churches, maintaining the crypt where the Holy Family is supposed to have stayed during their escape to

Egypt. The church's exquisite design represents centuries of spiritual significance.

Cultural Landmarks:

Coptic Museum: Immerse yourself in the history of Egypt's Christian community at the Coptic Museum. Housing a rich collection of manuscripts, textiles, and antiquities, it provides a comprehensive tour through Coptic art and culture.

Ben Ezra Synagogue: Witness the amicable coexistence of religions in the Ben Ezra Synagogue, previously a Coptic church. Its history demonstrates the dynamic cultural exchanges between Egypt's Jewish and Christian communities.

Religious Heritage:

Saint George's Church: Explore the spiritual ambiance of Saint George's Church, devoted to the dragon-slaying saint. The church's architecture and quiet atmosphere make it a refuge for contemplation.

Coptic Orthodox Patriarchate: Visit the seat of the Coptic Orthodox Pope at the Coptic Orthodox Patriarchate. The complex comprises the Cathedral of Saint Mark, affording a look into the ecclesiastical authority of the Coptic Church.

Historical Synthesis:

Roman Fortress of Babylon: Marvel at the relics of the Roman Fortress of Babylon, a historic monument that predates Islamic Cairo. Its strategic location played a vital role in the region's early Christian history.

Church of St. Sergius and Bacchus (Abu Serga): Admire the layers of history within the Church of St. Sergius and Bacchus, with its blend of Roman, Byzantine, and Coptic influences. The church serves as a tribute to Egypt's rich religious traditions.

Art and Architecture:

Coptic Icons: Appreciate the artistry of Coptic icons found in numerous churches. These elaborate paintings depict religious narratives and are fundamental parts of Coptic religious expression.

Architectural Diversity: Witness the different architectural styles, from ancient Coptic churches to well-preserved medieval monuments. Each building conveys a story of strength and permanence.

Local Insights:

Guided Tours: Consider joining guided tours to obtain deeper insights into the historical and cultural significance of each location. Knowledgeable guides can add context and deepen your understanding.

photographic Etiquette: When visiting churches and religious sites, be mindful of photographic etiquette and respect the hallowed environment.

Coptic Cairo welcomes you to walk the hallowed passageways of Egypt's Christian past. With its ancient churches, cultural treasures, and a blend of historical epochs, this region stands as a tribute to the lasting spirit of religious pluralism in Egypt.

2.5 The Egyptian Museum: A Treasure Trove of Antiquity

Step into the Egyptian Museum in Cairo, a world-renowned storehouse of the most extensive collection of ancient Egyptian artifacts. This landmark museum, located in the heart of the city, near Tahrir Square, takes you on an unrivalled journey through Egypt's rich and fascinating history.

Exploring Ancient Wonders:

King Tutankhamun's Treasures: Experience the wonder of King Tutankhamun's burial treasures, including his famous gold mask and sarcophagi. The young king's treasures provide insight into the grandeur and beauty of ancient Egyptian royal funerals.

Royal Mummies Hall: Marvel at the Royal Mummies Hall, where the preserved bodies of Egypt's greatest pharaohs, such Ramses II and Queen Hatshepsut, offer a direct link to the past. Witness the remarkable mummification procedures that have kept these monarchs intact for millennia.

Artifacts & Exhibits:

Statues and Sculptures: Admire an incredible collection of statues and sculptures, ranging from enormous to small, delicate pieces. These artworks reflect the creative progression and skill of ancient Egyptian culture.

Jewelry & Daily Life Objects: Explore exhibitions of fine jewelry, furniture, and items from everyday life, which provide an insight into the lifestyle, fashion, and customs of ancient Egyptians.

Historical Significance:

Old and Middle Kingdom Exhibits: Delve into the items from the Old and Middle Kingdoms, understanding the beginnings and growth of ancient Egyptian culture. These items disclose much about the social, political, and religious life of the time.

Ptolemaic and Roman Periods: Discover artifacts from the Ptolemaic and Roman periods, exhibiting the blend of

Egyptian, Greek, and Roman cultures. various artifacts demonstrate the vibrant and cosmopolitan nature of Egypt in various ages.

Educational Opportunities:

Guided Tours and Audio Guides: Take use of guided tours or audio guides to increase your comprehension of the exhibits. Expert guides provide context and fascinating facts about the museum's collection.

Educational Programs: The museum routinely conducts educational programs and special exhibitions, making it a great resource for both tourists and scholars.

Preservation and Innovation:

Conservation work: Learn about the museum's continuing conservation work, protecting these ancient treasures for future generations. The museum is a global leader in the field of archeological conservation.

Modernization Projects: The Egyptian Museum is continuously upgrading its exhibitions and visiting amenities, offering a rewarding experience for all.

Visitor Experience:

Interactive Displays: Some exhibitions incorporate interactive displays, letting visitors to engage more fully with ancient Egyptian history and culture.

Souvenir Shop & Amenities: Visit the museum's souvenir shop for souvenirs and publications. The museum also offers services like cafes and rest places for a comfortable visit.

The Egyptian Museum is not only a showcase of ancient riches; it's a portal to comprehending the depth and richness of Egyptian history. Whether you're a history enthusiast, an art lover, or simply inquisitive about the ancient past, the Egyptian Museum guarantees an unparalleled experience of one of humanity's most interesting civilizations.

Chapter 2

Cultural Insights

3.1 The Culinary Delights of Cairo: A Journey Through Egyptian Cuisine

Embark on a culinary trip in Cairo, where the colourful streets and marketplaces offer a tempting assortment of flavors, merging tradition and innovation to create a complex tapestry of Egyptian food.

Savoring Traditional Tastes:

Koshari - A Flavorful Medley: Indulge in Egypt's national cuisine, Koshari, a delectable combination of lentils, rice, pasta, and chickpeas, topped with spicy tomato sauce and crunchy fried onions. This rich dish epitomises the essence of Egyptian comfort food.

Ful Medames — Breakfast Staple: Start your day like a local with Ful Medames, a nutritious breakfast meal fashioned from slow-cooked fava beans seasoned with garlic, olive oil, and a variety of spices. Enjoy it with freshly made bread.

Street Food Delights:

Ta'ameya (Falafel): Take a stroll through Cairo's bustling streets and taste Ta'ameya, Egyptian falafel made with ground fava beans or chickpeas, combined with herbs and spices, then deep-fried to perfection. Pair it with tahini sauce for an authentic experience.

Hawawshi - Egyptian "Submarine" Sandwich: Sink your teeth into Hawawshi, a delectable street food sandwich consisting of spicy meat (typically beef or lamb) wrapped into flatbread and baked or grilled. It's a flavorsome and delightful on-the-go treat.

Iconic Dishes:

Molokhia Soup - A Green Delicacy: Sample Molokhia Soup, a nourishing green soup cooked from the leaves of the molokhia plant. Often prepared with garlic and coriander and served over rice or toast, it's a dish cherished for its particular taste.

Mahshi - packed Vegetables: Delight in Mahshi, a dish comprising vegetables like grape leaves, zucchini, and bell peppers packed with a seasoned mixture of rice, herbs, and sometimes minced beef. The outcome is a symphony of tastes in every bite.

Sweet Temptations:

Basbousa - Semolina Dessert: Treat your sweet craving to Basbousa, a classic semolina cake drenched in simple syrup and decorated with almonds or coconut. Its moist texture and sweetness make it a renowned dessert across Egypt.

Qatayef - Ramadan Delight: If your visit aligns with Ramadan, don't miss Qatayef, unique packed pancakes typically savoured during the holy month. These delectable delights can be filled with almonds, sweet cheese, or cream.

Tea Culture:

Egyptian Chai (Tea): Immerse yourself in Egyptian tea culture by sipping on classic chai. Whether it's the strong, dark brew or the milder 'Koshary' tea, tea establishments and street vendors offer a great getaway for tea connoisseurs.

Sahlab - Warming Winter Beverage: During colder months, appreciate Sahlab, a hot drink made from orchid root flour, milk, and other spices. Topped with nuts and coconut, it provides comfort and warmth.

Modern Culinary Scene:

Fusion Cafés and Restaurants: Cairo's culinary environment has welcomed innovation, with a wave of modern cafés and restaurants putting contemporary twists on traditional foods. Explore these venues to discover the evolving face of Egyptian cuisine.

Food Tours & Cooking courses: Enhance your culinary trip by taking food tours or cooking courses, where you may not only taste a variety of delicacies but also learn the art of preparing them from skilled chefs.

From old traditions passed down through generations to contemporary culinary trends, Cairo's food scene is a celebration of diversity and flavor. Allow your taste sensations to dance through the streets of Cairo, and you'll discover that Egyptian food is a true representation of the country's rich history and cultural tapestry.

3.2 Cairo's Markets and Bazaars: A Shopper's Delight

Dive into the rich tapestry of Cairo's markets and bazaars, where centuries-old traditions mingle with modern commerce, producing an unforgettable shopping experience. From busy souks to colourful street markets, Cairo invites you to explore its vast array of treasures.

1. Khan El Khalili: The Grand Bazaar

Historic Splendor: Wander through the small lanes of Khan El Khalili, Cairo's famed souk that dates back to the 14th century. Marvel at the complex building, embellished with beautiful mosaics and antique charm.

Traditional Crafts: Immerse yourself in the craftsmanship of local artists. Khan El Khalili is recognised for its fine handmade items, including delicately created jewelry, handwoven carpets, and traditional Islamic art.

Bargaining Skills: Engage in the art of bargaining as you navigate the labyrinthine market. From aromatic spices and vivid textiles to unusual souvenirs, hone your negotiation skills to score the greatest discounts.

2. Tahrir Square Souk: Modern Flair

Urban Elegance: Experience the modern heartbeat of Cairo in Tahrir Square Souk. This contemporary marketplace offers a mix of classic things and innovative, urban wares, reflecting Cairo's vibrant energy.

Fashion and Accessories: Indulge in the latest Egyptian fashion trends and accessories. From trendy apparel to locally crafted jewelry, Tahrir Square Souk is a paradise for fashion fans seeking a blend of heritage and modernity.

Culinary Delights: Explore markets loaded with aromatic spices, local specialties, and traditional desserts. The souk's gastronomic section allows you to take home a bit of Cairo's rich cuisine culture.

3. Wekalet El Balah: The Spice Market

Aromas and Colors: Delight your senses in Wekalet El Balah, the spice market where the air is saturated with the rich scents of exotic spices. Engage with local spice traders and explore a multitude of flavors.

Herbs and Medicinal Plants: Beyond spices, Wekalet El Balah is a treasure trove of herbs and medicinal plants. Explore the restorative powers of traditional Egyptian treatments and take home a piece of wellness.

Cultural Encounters: Interact with vendors who are passionate about conveying the cultural value of their products. Learn about the function of spices in Egyptian food and traditional medicine.

4. Street Markets in Islamic Cairo: Local Gems

real Local Life: Stroll through the picturesque streets of Islamic Cairo, where local street markets offer a real view into ordinary life. These marketplaces are perfect for individuals seeking real, locally sourced products.

Handicrafts and Artifacts: Discover hidden treasures, including handcrafted crafts, old artifacts, and antique antiques. The street markets in Islamic Cairo are a refuge for collectors and people interested about preserving Egypt's cultural heritage.

Tea and foods: Take a stop at one of the classic tea booths and sample local foods. Engage in casual chats with residents, getting insights into the everyday rhythms of Cairo's historic neighborhoods.

5. Asfour El Nil: Jewelry Haven

Elegant Adornments: Explore the sparkling world of Asfour El Nil, a jewelry bazaar famed for its stunning designs. From traditional gold and silver pieces to innovative interpretations, this market caters to varied tastes.

Customization Options: Immerse yourself in the art of jewelry manufacturing. Many stores in Asfour El Nil provide customising options, allowing you to design a unique piece that encapsulates your Cairo experience.

Cultural Symbolism: Learn about the cultural importance of different jewelry types. From pieces inspired by ancient Egyptian motifs to contemporary designs influenced by Cairo's cosmopolitan ambiance, each item tells a story.

Cairo's markets and bazaars draw you into a world where the past and present mingle, giving a kaleidoscope of colors, scents, and sounds. Whether you're seeking traditional crafts, modern fashion, or a taste of local cuisine, these colourful marketplaces urge you to immerse yourself in the rich fabric of Cairo's cultural and commercial legacy.

3.3 Celebrating Egyptian Festivals: A Kaleidoscope of Culture and Joy

Egyptian festivals are a dynamic representation of the nation's unique cultural tapestry, merging old traditions with contemporary celebrations. Participating in these events offers a unique glimpse into the heart and spirit of Egypt, its people, and their traditions.

1. Ramadan and Eid al-Fitr

Spiritual contemplation: Ramadan, the holy month of fasting, is a time of spiritual contemplation and community. Experience the festive atmosphere in Cairo as the city comes alive with special evening dinners (Iftar) and social events.

Eid al-Fitr Celebrations: Marking the conclusion of Ramadan, Eid al-Fitr is a festive occasion filled with food, family gatherings, and charity. The streets of Cairo are decked with decorations, and people exchange gifts and well wishes.

2. Sham El-Nessim: Welcoming Spring

Ancient Origins: Sham El-Nessim, an ancient Egyptian festival, celebrates the entrance of spring. This official holiday, falling on the day after Coptic Easter, is a time for family picnics and outdoor activities.

Traditional dishes: Enjoy traditional dishes like feseekh (salted fish), lettuce, and colored boiled eggs. These foods are a vital component of the celebration, signifying life, rebirth, and the wealth of the Nile.

3. Cairo International Film Festival

Cinematic Excellence: As one of the oldest and most prestigious film festivals in the Arab world, the Cairo International Film Festival shows a varied spectrum of films, from local productions to international cinema.

Star-studded Events: Rub shoulders with filmmakers, actors, and industry experts. Attend screenings, workshops, and panel discussions that highlight the art of cinema and cultural exchange.

4. Moulid El-Nabi: The Prophet's Birthday

Spiritual Celebration: Moulid El-Nabi honours the birthday of the Prophet Muhammad. It's a time for religious gatherings, storytelling, and special prayers in mosques across Cairo.

Festive Atmosphere: Streets and homes are decked with lights and banners. Enjoy the festive environment, complete with traditional treats like sugared almonds and halawet el-moulid.

5. Sphinx Festival: Cultural Fusion

Artistic Showcase: The Sphinx Festival at Giza is a wonderful celebration of Egyptian and other cultures. It incorporates music, dancing, art workshops, and historical lectures, set against the backdrop of the renowned Sphinx and pyramids.

Cultural Exchange: Participate in workshops and events that emphasise the blend of ancient and modern Egyptian culture. This event offers a rare opportunity to engage with artists and intellectuals from around the world.

6. Coptic Christmas: A Winter Celebration

Religious Observance: Celebrated on January 7th, Coptic Christmas is a significant holiday for Egypt's Christian population. Attend the Midnight Mass at Cairo's antique Coptic churches for a really mystical experience.

celebratory Foods: Post-service, families congregate for a celebratory lunch, breaking the Advent fast. Traditional foods like Fatta (a pork and rice dish) are offered, along with special Christmas bread.

Egyptian holidays are not merely festivities; they provide a window into the essence of the nation. They merge the holy and the secular, the old and the modern, generating experiences that are both distinctly Egyptian and universally human. As a visitor, partaking in these festivals allows you to connect closely with Egypt's history, religion, and contemporary culture.

3.4 Traditional Arts & Crafts: The Essence of Egypt's Artistic Heritage

Egypt's traditional arts and crafts are a colourful tribute to the country's rich cultural past. These crafts are not simply plain things; they embody the skills, tales, and traditions passed down through generations. Exploring these arts provides a broader appreciation of Egypt's past and the ingenuity of its people.

1. Papyrus Making: The Ancient Paper

Historical Significance: Papyrus was the ancient Egyptians' innovation for paper, vital for chronicling history and culture. Today, craftsmen keep this practice alive, creating exquisite artworks and calligraphy on papyrus.

Artistic Process: Visit a papyrus institute in Cairo to experience the delicate process of changing the papyrus plant into a writing surface. These courses generally demonstrate the skill of papyrus painting, using traditional Egyptian designs and hieroglyphs.

2. Alabaster Sculpture: Stone of Light

Centuries-Old Craftsmanship: Alabaster, a translucent stone, has been utilised for millennia in Egypt for crafting statues, vases, and other beautiful things. Artisans in regions like Luxor and Aswan are famous for their skill in crafting this delicate material.

Unique Souvenirs: Alabaster workshops offer a range of wonderful items, from small trinkets to huge vases, each piece handcrafted and unique. These products make for memorable mementos, encapsulating the essence of Egyptian craftsmanship.

3. Ceramics and Pottery: Shaping the Nile's Clay

Ancient Techniques: Egyptian pottery dates back to prehistoric times. Artisans in communities like Fustat (Old Cairo) still use traditional processes to manufacture pottery, drawing inspiration from historical designs and methods.

Diverse Styles: Explore the variety of Egyptian ceramics, from the blue and white patterns influenced by Ottoman and Islamic art to more contemporary designs. These pieces illustrate the synthesis of many cultural and historical elements in Egyptian art.

4. Hand-Woven Textiles: The Fabric of Life

Weaving Heritage: Textile weaving, especially in locations like Akhmim and Siwa, is a centuries-old practice. These tribes make superb hand-woven fabrics, including cotton, linen, and wool.

Cultural Patterns: Discover the spectrum of Egyptian textiles, from Bedouin-inspired designs to Coptic and Islamic motifs. Traditional looms are still used to manufacture everything from clothes and tapestries to beautiful home materials.

5. Glass Blowing: A Delicate Art

Ancient Art Form: Glass making in Egypt has ancient beginnings. Today's artisans in Cairo and beyond continue to pursue this captivating trade, creating both classic and modern glassware.

Artisanal Creations: Watch glassblowers at work, sculpting molten glass into exquisite shapes. The final products, including lamps, ornaments, and dinnerware, highlight the beauty and skill required in this technique.

6. Metalwork: Intricate Craftsmanship

Legacy of Skill: Egyptian metalwork, particularly in copper and brass, is famed for its elaborate designs. Artisans in Khan El Khalili and other old markets excel at making detailed metal sculptures.

Functional Art: From ornate lanterns and delicate trays to jewelry and ornamental plates, the spectrum of metal crafts is enormous. These sculptures generally contain Islamic calligraphy, geometric designs, and elements from nature.

By discovering Egypt's traditional arts and crafts, visitors not only gain insight into the country's artistic past but also help the local artists who are the caretakers of these age-old talents. These crafts are more than souvenirs; they are tangible connections to Egypt's history and a witness to its everlasting cultural richness.

3.5 Navigating Cairo's Contemporary Art Scene: A Blend of Tradition and Modernity

Cairo's contemporary art scene is a vibrant and growing arena, where traditional Egyptian aesthetics intermingle with current and worldwide artistic expressions. This bustling environment offers a unique perspective on the country's cultural and social evolution, reflecting the thoughts and aspirations of its current artists. For art connoisseurs and casual viewers alike, touring Cairo's modern art environment is an enlightening experience.

1. Art Galleries and Exhibition Spaces: The Pulse of Modern Creativity

Diverse Venues: Cairo is home to a diversity of art galleries, from well-established institutions to avant-garde locations. Galleries including Townhouse, Gypsum, and Zamalek Art Gallery present works ranging from painting and sculpture to multimedia installations.

Cultural Exchanges: These galleries regularly feature exhibitions involving both local and foreign artists, promoting a cultural discussion and presenting fresh insights on global and regional issues.

2. Street Art: The City's Canvas

Urban Expression: The streets of Cairo have become a canvas for local painters, with murals and graffiti covering the city's walls. This street art often reflects social and political concerns, allowing insight into the public mentality.

Walking Tours: Guided walking tours are provided, taking tourists through neighborhoods rich in street art, notably Mohamed Mahmoud Street, providing context and background on the artworks and their creators.

3. Art Festivals and Biennales: Celebrating Contemporary Arts

Annual Events: Cairo holds many art festivals and biennales, such as the Cairo International Biennale and the Downtown Contemporary Arts Festival (D-CAF). These events span a wide range of artistic disciplines and draw artists and viewers from around the world.

creative Platforms: These festivals provide a venue for creative artistic expressions and partnerships, featuring cutting-edge performances, visual arts, and digital media.

4. Artistic Workshops and Residencies: Nurturing Talent

Learning Opportunities: Various cultural centers and art places in Cairo provide workshops and residencies for artists. These initiatives encourage experimentation and give resources for artists to enhance their talents and participate with the local art community.

Interactive Experiences: Visitors can often engage in these workshops, obtaining hands-on experience in diverse art genres and interacting with local artists.

5. Contemporary Art Museums: A Window to Modern Art

Institutional Collections: Museums like the Museum of Modern Egyptian Art in Cairo display works by important Egyptian painters from the 20th century to the present, presenting a historical perspective on the growth of modern Egyptian art.

Curatorial Narratives: These museums regularly curate thematic exhibitions, allowing visitors to explore various facets of contemporary art in Egypt, from abstract movements to social realism.

6. Performance Art: Theatrical and Dance Innovations

Dynamic Performances: Cairo's current performance art scene includes experimental theater and contemporary dance, often produced in alternative locations and cultural centers.

Cross-Cultural Collaborations: These performances sometimes entail collaborations between Egyptian and international artists, generating a combination of styles and themes that communicate to a worldwide audience.

Navigating Cairo's modern art scene is an investigation of the city's heartbeat, where tradition and innovation combine. This voyage not only uncovers the artistic abilities of Egypt's modern innovators but also provides a window into the rich and growing cultural landscape of this historic metropolis.

Chapter 3

Modern Cairo

4.1 New Cairo's Architectural Wonders: A Meeting of Modernity and Elegance

With its combination of modern design and a hint of classic grandeur, New Cairo exemplifies Egypt's dedication to modern urban development. Since its founding in the latter half of the twentieth century, the neighbourhood has grown into a centre of cutting-edge technology and culture. Architectural wonders of New Cairo, when explored, reveal a scene where modern style blends with practical city life.

One, the Cairo Festival City Mall: A Contemporary Shopping Extravaganza

A haven for retail therapy, the Cairo Festival City Mall is a work of art in and of itself. Open areas, natural light, and water features are all part of the mall's architecture, making it a pleasant place to shop.

Contemporary Aesthetics: The mall highlights current Egyptian design characteristics, and its varied selection of shops, restaurants, and entertainment venues make it a dynamic center for social and retail activity.

Educational Excellence in Design at the New Cairo Campus of the American University in Cairo (AUC)

Academic Oasis: The AUC New Cairo Campus is a blend of educational purpose and architectural magnificence. Modern architecture, verdant landscaping, and state-of-the-art facilities characterise the campus.

Practices that Promote Sustainability: Eco-friendly design features, energy-efficient technologies, and a dedication to environmental responsibility are all part of the sustainability focus.

3. Cairo Opera House: Cultural Grandeur in Contemporary Form

Architectural Symmetry: The Cairo Opera House in New Cairo is a cultural icon, with a design that mixes classical elements with contemporary aesthetics. The building's grandeur is a great backdrop for the numerous performances it presents.

Cultural Hub: Beyond its architectural significance, the Cairo Opera House plays a key role in fostering the arts, making it a cultural centre inside New Cairo.

4. Egyptian Grand Museum: A Monument to Ancient and Modern

Majestic Presence: The Egyptian Grand Museum, positioned against the backdrop of the Giza Pyramids, is an architectural masterpiece in New Cairo. Its huge edifice not only stores a rich trove of ancient treasures but also reflects modern design on a massive scale.

Historical Integration: The museum's design naturally blends with its historical surroundings, creating a harmonious connection between ancient Egypt and the present.

5. Dusit Thani LakeView Cairo: Luxury Living with a Panoramic View

Urban Oasis: Dusit Thani LakeView Cairo is a superb example of architectural elegance in New Cairo. The hotel's architecture stresses both richness and comfort, allowing inhabitants and guests a hideaway in the midst of the metropolis.

Scenic Splendor: Its strategic location affords panoramic views of the surrounding lakes and greenery, improving the overall experience of staying in this architectural jewel.

6. Cairo Festival Tower: Skyline Sophistication

Vertical Elegance: The Cairo Festival Tower is a significant component of New Cairo's skyline. This architectural masterpiece houses a blend of residential, business, and leisure facilities, with a design that complements the district's multicultural environment.

Skyline Integration: The tower's design lends a touch of modernism to the skyline, becoming a visual representation of New Cairo's urban expansion.

7. Katameya Dunes: Opulent Residences in Nature's Embrace

Golf and Residences Katameya Dunes is a residential development that intertwines luxurious living with natural scenery. The architectural layout mixes residential spaces with a world-class golf course, producing a harmonic blend of urbanity and nature.

Community Living: The design emphasizes community living, with features that appeal to both recreation and relaxation, making it a remarkable architectural venture in New Cairo.

Exploring the architectural marvels of New Cairo uncovers a cityscape that not only fits the demands of modern urban living but also honours the rich history and cultural heritage of Egypt. Each structure contributes to the district's charm, producing a balanced blend of contemporary beauty and timeless sophistication.

4.2 Cairo's Green Spaces and Parks: Urban Oases Amidst the Bustle

Cairo, a bustling metropolis, embraces the need for peaceful sanctuaries inside its urban framework. The city boasts a plethora of green spaces and parks, giving residents and visitors alike with havens of serenity despite the busy metropolitan atmosphere. Discover the verdant treasures that contribute to Cairo's combination of urban vitality and natural peace.

Al-Azhar Park: Historic Beauty Reimagined

Oasis in Old Cairo: Al-Azhar Park stands as a magnificent example to urban regeneration. Once a landfill, it has been turned into a verdant oasis with gardens, water features, and stunning views of historic Cairo.

Cultural Hub: Beyond its greenery, the park conducts cultural activities and gives a location for peaceful reflection, making it a varied getaway.

Al-Azhar Park Lakes: Tranquil Waters in the Heart of Cairo

Serenity by the Lakes: Adjacent to Al-Azhar Park, the lakes offer calm settings. Visitors can enjoy boat excursions, strolls around the lakeside, and moments of quiet in this exquisite location.

gorgeous Landscapes: The lakes enhance the overall splendour of Al-Azhar Park, offering a gorgeous backdrop to the historic structures visible from its borders.

Al Montaza Park: Coastal Serenity

Seaside Bliss: Al Montaza Park, situated along the Mediterranean coast, offers a refreshing blend of vegetation and seaside charm. Palatial gardens, strolling paths, and access to the seaside make it a wonderful vacation.

Historic Palaces: Within the park, tourists can explore historical palaces, giving a touch of regal charm to the park's natural beauty.

Family Park (Al Azhar Park Extension): Recreation for All

Playful Escape: Catering to families, the Family Park extension of Al-Azhar Park features playgrounds, open spaces, and recreational facilities. It's a great area for families to unwind amidst nature.

Community Gathering: The park encourages a sense of community, drawing residents and families seeking a common space for pleasure and relaxation.

Orman Botanical Garden: Botanical Diversity in Giza

Floral Paradise: Orman Botanical Garden, located in Giza, is a refuge for plant enthusiasts. Its vast assortment of plants, themed gardens, and serene walks create a unique botanical experience.

Educational Initiatives: The garden acts as an educational resource, encouraging awareness about plant species and conservation, making it an enriching experience for all ages.

Giza Zoo: Wildlife Amidst Greenery

Zoological Oasis: Giza Zoo, one of the oldest in the world, mixes lush green settings with a wide array of fauna. Visitors can enjoy a day surrounded by nature while watching a variety of animal species.

Conservation Focus: The zoo participates in conservation initiatives and educational activities, emphasizing the value of biodiversity and environmental awareness.

Fish Garden (Azbakeya Wall Garden): A Historic Oasis

Historical Charm: The Fish Garden, located within the old Azbakeya Wall, is a hidden gem. Its ponds, bridges, and shaded spaces offer a serene escape, enabling tourists to travel back in time.

Architectural Heritage: The garden's design reflects historical influences, giving a unique environment that blends natural beauty with architectural appeal.

International Park: Global Flair in Cairo

Cultural Fusion: International Park, as the name says, incorporates many themes from throughout the world. Each part symbolises a different country, allowing tourists a global experience within Cairo.

Culinary Exploration: The park often holds food festivals and cultural activities, turning visits into immersive voyages of world discovery.

Cairo's green spaces and parks serve as crucial lungs for the city, delivering relief from its hectic pace. Whether seeking historical charm, beach peace, or a worldwide retreat, these urban oases contribute to Cairo's attractiveness as a city where nature and culture coexist harmoniously.

4.3 The Nile Corniche: Cairo's Waterfront Promenade - A Riverside Reverie

The Nile Corniche, a bustling promenade spanning along the Nile River in Cairo, gives a unique perspective of the city where the timeless river meets modern urbanity. As a beloved attraction for both locals and tourists, it delivers a lively combination of leisure, culture, and scenic beauty, representing the essence of Cairo in its riverine backdrop.

Scenic Strolls and Riverside Views:

Panoramic Vistas: The Corniche offers stunning vistas of the Nile, a fantastic setting for leisurely strolls. The ever-changing riverscape, with historic feluccas and contemporary vessels, forms a lovely scene.

Sunset Magic: As the sun sets, the Nile transforms into a palette of hues, making evening walks particularly enchanting.

Cultural Fusion and Entertainment:

Cafés & Restaurants: Lining the Corniche are several dining facilities, ranging from typical Egyptian coffee shops to sophisticated restaurants, serving both local and international cuisines with Nile views.

Entertainment Venues: The region buzzes with life, featuring a range of entertainment alternatives including live music, cultural events, and seasonal festivals.

Felucca Rides: A Traditional Experience:

Time-Honored Tradition: Feluccas, traditional Egyptian sailboats, offer calm river cruises. These calm cruises provide a unique approach to enjoy the Nile's splendour.

Nighttime Cruises: Evening felucca cruises are particularly popular, allowing a calm getaway from the city's hustle while admiring the lit skyline.

Jogging and Cycling Paths:

Active Lifestyle: For individuals seeking physical activity, the Corniche provides running and cycling trails. The riverfront walk offers a pleasant and encouraging atmosphere for exercising.

Wellness in the City: This blending of greenery and paths encourages wellness and a healthy lifestyle amidst urban surroundings.

Historical and Modern Landmarks:

Architectural Wonders: The Corniche is lined with major structures, including the Cairo Tower, a symbol of contemporary Egypt, and other old buildings showing architectural diversity.

Luxury Hotels and Businesses: The neighbourhood is also home to various luxury hotels and corporate facilities, contributing to its prominence as a prominent commercial hub.

Environmental and Urban Development:

Renovation Projects: Recent efforts focus on reviving and expanding the Corniche, boosting its appeal and accessibility.

Green Initiatives: Environmental considerations are increasingly impacting the development, attempting to balance urban growth with ecological sustainability.

Community Gatherings and Social Interactions:

Social Hub: The Corniche works as a social hub, where people from all walks of life converge, reflecting Cairo's broad social fabric.

Family-Friendly Spaces: With spaces dedicated for children's play and family picnics, it is a favourite weekend destination for families.

Artistic & Creative Spaces:

Art works: The promenade often incorporates temporary art works and exhibitions, providing an artistic component to the riverbank experience.

Creative Inspiration: Artists and photographers commonly assemble here, lured by the Corniche's scenic and cultural diversity.

The Nile Corniche is more than just a waterfront promenade; it is a vibrant artery of Cairo, capturing the city's pulse. It offers an area where history, culture, leisure, and natural beauty merge, allowing inhabitants and visitors a comprehensive experience by the beautiful Nile.

4.4 Nightlife & Entertainment: Cairo's Vibrant Nocturnal Tapestry

When the sun sets over Cairo, a new energy emerges, and the city's nightlife comes alive with a kaleidoscope of entertainment possibilities. From sophisticated cafés and exciting nightclubs to cultural shows, Cairo offers a broad and dynamic nocturnal tapestry that caters to every taste and inclination.

Rooftop Retreats and Skyline Soirees:

Panoramic Perspectives: Cairo's skyline is a canvas of glittering lights, and rooftop locations provide a stunning backdrop. Enjoy a beverage with views of prominent sights like the Cairo Tower or the lit Nile.

Eclectic Nightclubs and Music Venues:

Beats of the Night: Cairo's nightlife is known for its lively music scene. Trendy nightclubs host local and international DJs, blasting everything from techno and house to Arabic sounds. Live music venues exhibit varied genres, gratifying music enthusiasts.

Cultural Extravaganza:

Traditional Performances: Immerse yourself in Egypt's cultural diversity with traditional music and dance performances. Some places present engaging concerts, featuring belly dancing, folk music, and classical Egyptian compositions.

Theatrical Arts: Explore theaters showcasing plays, current performances, and stand-up comedy, delivering a blend of entertainment and cultural participation.

Nile Cruises and Dinner Experiences:

Floating Feasts: Embark on a magnificent Nile cruise, where dinner is complemented by the smooth flow of the river and the sparkling city lights. These cruises offer a romantic and relaxed way to spend the evening.

Bazaars and Night Markets:

Nocturnal Shopping: Experience the vivid atmosphere of Cairo's night marketplaces and bazaars. Some stay open late, letting you engage in evening shopping for local crafts, spices, and souvenirs.

Late-Night Cafés and Shisha Lounges:

Caffeine and Conversations: Cairo's café culture goes into the late hours. Enjoy a cup of creamy Arabic coffee or a calming tea in one of the numerous quiet cafés. Shisha lounges offer a relaxing backdrop for talks beneath the sky.

Themed Bars and Speakeasies:

Quirky Themes: Explore themed bars and hidden speakeasies that add an element of mystery and variety to the evening experience. From nostalgic motifs to dramatic backdrops, there's a place for every mood.

Artistic Hotspots:

Galleries After Dark: Some art galleries extend their hours for special nighttime activities, allowing art fans to view exhibitions and connect with fellow patrons in a more private atmosphere.

Late-Night Eateries:

Gastronomic Delights: Cairo's culinary scene doesn't slumber. Late-night cafes and street food booths serve up scrumptious delicacies, ensuring that hunger pains are satisfied long into the night.

Safe and Dynamic Atmosphere:

Security Measures: The city lays a significant focus on safety, with well-lit locations and heightened security, guaranteeing that residents and visitors may enjoy the nightlife with peace of mind.

Diverse Crowds: Cairo's nightlife welcomes a diverse crowd, creating a vibrant and welcoming setting where individuals from all backgrounds join together to celebrate.

Cairo's nightlife isn't just a sequence of events; it's a reflection of the city's energy and perseverance. Whether you seek throbbing beats, cultural immersion, or a quiet riverbank meal, Cairo's after-dark attractions promise an unforgettable experience in the heart of Egypt.

4.5 Dining Out in Cairo: From Street Food to Fine Dining

Cairo's culinary scene is a compelling trip that caters to a spectrum of tastes, from the olfactory joys of street food carts to the polished ambiance of upmarket dining venues. Discover the unique gastronomic environment that distinguishes Cairo's eating experience.

Street Food Extravaganza:

Aromas of the Alleyways: Dive into Cairo's bustling streets to experience the colourful tapestry of street food. From koshari, a native staple of lentils and rice, to ta'ameya (falafel) and kofta, the multitude of flavors reflects the city's unique culinary tradition.

Local Markets and Food Bazaars:

Marketplace Marvels: Explore traditional markets like Khan El Khalili, where street sellers and food booths provide a choice of local specialties. Sample exotic fruits, nuts, and freshly squeezed liquids for a true taste of Cairo.

Egyptian Staples in Cafés:

Café Culture: Cairo's cafés are not simply about coffee; they are social hubs. Indulge in classic Egyptian coffee or tea accompanied by mezze, pastries, or sweets, creating an ideal backdrop for unhurried talks.

Nile-side Dining:

Riverfront Repasts: Enjoy a dinner with a view along the Nile. Riverside restaurants offer a serene backdrop, allowing you to taste Egyptian food while the river slowly runs beside you.

Fine Dining with a Twist:

Modern Egyptian Fusion: Upscale restaurants in Cairo merge traditional Egyptian ingredients with current culinary techniques. Experience a new twist on classics, delivered with creative flare and gastronomic delicacy.

International Cuisine Hubs:

Global Gastronomy: Cairo's global nature is reflected in its numerous dining alternatives. Explore restaurants serving international cuisines, from Mediterranean and Italian to Asian fusion, pleasing diverse palates.

Historic Dining Establishments:

Timeless Elegance: Step inside historic establishments that have lasted the test of time, where opulent décor and classic recipes create an ambiance that transports diners to a bygone period.

Seafood Delights:

Mediterranean Bounty: Given Cairo's proximity to the Mediterranean, seafood aficionados can indulge in a range of fresh catches. Seafood restaurants serve scrumptious dishes created with an emphasis on quality and flavor.

Rooftop Retreats:

Sky-high Gastronomy: Elevate your dining experience at rooftop restaurants, where panoramic views of the city complement superb cuisine. Whether at sunset or under the stars, these venues offer a spectacular culinary excursion.

Culinary Events & Food Festivals:

Feasts for the Foodie: Participate in Cairo's culinary events and food festivals, where chefs demonstrate their talents, and tourists may indulge in a gastronomic trip featuring a vast diversity of cuisines.

Dessert Destinations:

Sweet Confections: End your gastronomic excursion on a sweet note. Cairo's dessert shops and patisseries manufacture delectable delicacies, from traditional Egyptian sweets to cosmopolitan pastries.

Accessible Eateries for All:

Cairo's dining scene caters to varied budgets and interests, guaranteeing that everyone, from locals to international guests, can find a pleasant and delicious dinner.

Dining out in Cairo is not just a meal; it's an immersion into a culinary tradition that has grown over generations. Whether you're tasting street-side pleasures, embracing modern gastronomy, or enjoying a cultural dining experience, Cairo welcomes you to embark on a savoury trip through its diverse and wonderful food choices.

Chapter 4

Adventures in Cairo

5.1 Felucca Rides on the Nile

A vacation to Cairo would be incomplete without enjoying the timeless charm of a Felucca sail on the Nile. These classic Egyptian sailing boats give a quiet and charming approach to see the river's beauty and the city's landscape. Here's all you need to know about this unique Egyptian experience:

Historical Significance:

Ancient Traditions: Feluccas have been a feature of Egyptian river life for millennia, formerly the major mode of transport down the Nile. Today, they offer a historical perspective on Egypt's relationship with its life-giving river.

The Felucca Experience:

Tranquil Sailing: Without motors, Feluccas give a tranquil, eco-friendly sailing experience. The calm sound of the wind in the sail and the gentle movement of the boat give a peaceful respite from the bustling city.

Best Time for Rides:

Sunset Serenity: The most popular time for a Felucca ride is around sunset when the sky's changing colors offer a magnificent backdrop against the city skyline and the peaceful Nile waterways.

Booking a Ride:

Flexible Options: Felucca rides can be hired along the Corniche or through hotels and travel firms. Rides normally last for an hour, although longer journeys can be arranged.

Customized Trips:

Personalized Journeys: Whether you're searching for a romantic outing, a family adventure, or a quiet reflective cruise, Felucca captains can adapt the experience to your tastes.

Cultural Insights:

Engage with Locals: Many Felucca captains like sharing stories and insights about the Nile and Cairo, offering a unique cultural exchange opportunity.

Nighttime Cruises:

Starry Skies: For a new perspective, consider a night cruise. The lights of Cairo reflected on the river beneath the starry sky provide a magical and unique experience.

Safety and Comfort:

Preparedness is Key: While Feluccas are normally safe, it's advisable to verify the boat's condition and ensure life jackets are accessible, especially for non-swimmers and youngsters.

Catered Rides:

Dining on the Nile: Some Felucca trips provide the option of dining onboard, with numerous food and beverage options, complementing the experience with the flavour of local cuisine.

Photography Opportunities:

Capture the Moment: The Felucca journey affords several photo opportunities, from sweeping cityscapes to close-up shots of life along the Nile.

Eco-Friendly Aspect:

Sustainable Tourism: Opting for a Felucca trip helps eco-friendly tourism, as these sailboats do not contaminate the Nile with noise or pollutants.

Accessibility:

For Everyone: Feluccas are generally accessible for most people, however boarding and disembarking may require assistance for those with mobility concerns.

A Felucca ride on the Nile is more than just a tour; it's a trip into the heart of Egypt's culture and history. As you glide along the river, enveloped by the lovely breeze and surrounded by the sights and sounds of Cairo, you share in an experience that ties you to the ageless spirit of the Nile.

5.2 Camel and Horseback Tours

Embark on a unique adventure through the bustling streets and ancient wonders of Cairo with Camel and Horseback Tours. Whether exploring the iconic pyramids or meandering through historic districts, these tours offer an authentic and memorable way to experience the city. Here's what you can expect:

Pyramids Exploration:

Iconic Landmarks: Ride a camel or horse to explore the awe-inspiring Pyramids of Giza. This classic mode of transportation provides a connection to ancient times and offers a distinctive view of these architectural marvels.

Giza Plateau Ride:

Panoramic Views: Enjoy a leisurely ride around the Giza Plateau, marveling at the pyramids and capturing breathtaking panoramic views of these ancient wonders.

Professional Guides:

Experienced Handlers: Knowledgeable guides and handlers accompany the tours, ensuring a safe and informative experience. They are often well-versed in the history and significance of the sites visited.

Customized Routes:

Tailored Experiences: Tours can be customized based on your preferences and interests. Whether you prefer a direct route to the pyramids or a more scenic journey, the experience is adaptable to your desires.

Historical Districts:

Old Cairo Exploration: Explore the historic districts of Old Cairo, such as Islamic Cairo and Coptic Cairo, on horseback or camelback. This allows for a unique perspective as you navigate narrow streets and uncover hidden gems.

Flexible Duration:

Short Rides or Day Tours: Tours can vary in duration, from short rides around specific landmarks to full-day excursions exploring multiple sites. Choose an option that suits your schedule and energy levels.

Cultural Immersion:

Local Interactions: Engage with locals as you traverse different neighborhoods. This mode of travel often invites friendly exchanges with residents, providing insights into daily life in Cairo.

Photography Opportunities:

Capture the Moment: Riding on camelback or horseback offers excellent photo opportunities. Capture the essence of your journey with shots of ancient architecture, vibrant street scenes, and your unique perspective from atop these majestic animals.

Training and Guidance:

For All Skill Levels: Whether you're a seasoned rider or a first-timer, tours typically accommodate all skill levels. Guides provide basic training, ensuring a comfortable and enjoyable experience for everyone.

Comfort and Safety:

Well-Cared-for Animals: Reputable tour operators prioritize the well-being of their animals, ensuring they are well-cared for and in good health. Safety measures, such as helmets, may be provided.

Booking Options:

Through Tour Operators: Camel and Horseback Tours can be booked through various tour operators in Cairo, often including transportation, guides, and sometimes meals, providing a hassle-free experience.

Group or Private Tours:

Personalized Experiences: Choose between joining a group tour for a social experience or opting for a private tour for a more intimate and personalized adventure.

Discover the charm of Cairo in a truly distinctive way with Camel and Horseback Tours, where every ride becomes a journey through history, culture, and the vibrant spirit of this captivating city.

5.3 Hot Air Balloon Rides Over the City

Elevate your Cairo experience to new heights with Hot Air Balloon Rides, giving a spectacular and calm journey above the city's prominent sites. Here's what awaiting you on this fantastic adventure:

Aerial Panoramas:

360-Degree Views: Soar high above Cairo for breathtaking 360-degree panoramas of the cityscape. From the sprawling metropolitan environment to historic structures, behold the splendour of Cairo from a unique perspective point.

Sunrise Serenity:

Early Morning Excursions: Most hot air balloon trips take place during the early morning hours, delivering a magnificent sunrise experience. Watch as the first rays of day illuminate the city and its ancient beauties.

Pyramids & Sphinx Views:

Iconic Landmarks: Drift gently over the Pyramids of Giza and the Sphinx, capturing incomparable vistas of these eternal emblems of Egypt. The lovely dawn light increases the grandeur of these old monuments.

Professional Balloon Pilots:

Expert Guidance: Experienced and licensed balloon pilots lead the expedition, ensuring a safe and entertaining journey. Their familiarity of the region gives crucial insights as they navigate the balloon across the Cairo skyline.

Quiet and Peaceful Atmosphere:

Tranquil Experience: Unlike other modes of travel, hot air balloon trips offer a pleasant and quiet ambiance, creating a peaceful environment to absorb the surroundings without the hum of engines.

Landmarks from Above:

City Highlights: Glide over Cairo's architectural masterpieces, including mosques, palaces, and the flowing Nile River. The bird's-eye view provides a fresh appreciation for the city's rich history and different communities.

Photography Opportunities:

Capture Magical Moments Bring your camera to capture the magical moments from above. The beautiful morning light, paired with the unique perspective, gives stunning photo chances that will become cherished memories.

Group or Private Flights:

Personalized Experiences: Hot air balloon operators generally provide both group and private flight choices. Choose a group excursion for a social adventure or choose for a private flight for a more intimate voyage with loved ones.

Champagne Toast Celebration:

Post-Flight Tradition: Many hot air balloon tours conclude with a traditional champagne toast, toasting the successful journey. It's a lovely way to end up the journey with fellow participants.

Booking Considerations:

Advance arrangements Due to the popularity of hot air balloon trips, it's suggested to make advance arrangements. Check with trustworthy operators for availability and package alternatives.

Weather-Dependent Excursions:

Optimal Conditions: Hot air balloon rides are weather-dependent, and operators prioritize safety. Be prepared for possible rescheduling according on weather conditions, with clear mornings frequently delivering the finest experiences.

Experience Cairo in a really magical way with Hot Air Balloon Rides, where the silence of the skies and the spectacular sights create an experience that lasts a lifetime. It's a one-of-a-kind adventure that adds a touch of enchantment to your exploration of this dynamic city.

5.4 Day Trips to Ancient Sites

Exploring Cairo offers a unique doorway to Egypt's ancient history, and day visits to neighbouring historic monuments are a must for any traveler. These trips provide an opportunity to delve deeper into Egypt's rich heritage and explore the treasures beyond the city limits. Here are some of the most captivating day trips to consider:

Saqqara and the Step Pyramid:

History Comes Alive: Just a short drive from Cairo, Saqqara is home to the Step Pyramid of Djoser, one of the first large-scale stone monuments in Egypt. This pyramid indicates a key evolution in ancient Egyptian buildings.

Necropolis Exploration: The site also comprises many tombs and burial grounds, allowing an insight into ancient burial rituals and beliefs.

Memphis: The Ancient Capital:

Once a Thriving Metropolis: Memphis, the ancient capital of Egypt, located near Saqqara. Although much of it is in ruins, the site nonetheless gives insight into the grandeur of the city that once was a cultural and political capital.

Statue of Ramses II: Among the highlights is the huge statue of Ramses II, demonstrating the brilliance of ancient Egyptian sculpture.

Dahshur: Red and Bent Pyramids:

Architectural Marvels: Located a bit further from Saqqara, Dahshur is notable for two remarkable pyramids - the Red Pyramid and the Bent Pyramid. Both offer a different perspective on the evolution of pyramid construction.

Less Crowded Experience: Dahshur receives less tourists, allowing a more calm and intimate interaction with ancient Egypt.

Alexandria: The Mediterranean Jewel:

Cultural Blend: Although a lengthier travel, Alexandria is a magnificent seaside city with a rich history integrating Egyptian, Greek, and Roman civilizations. Key sites include the Catacombs of Kom El Shoqafa, the Roman Amphitheatre, and the present Bibliotheca Alexandrina.

Mediterranean Charm: The city also offers a refreshing change of scenery with its Mediterranean vibe, seafood cuisine, and coastal promenades.

Luxor: The World's Greatest Open-Air Museum (Overnight Recommended):

Temple Extravaganza: While more than a day trip, Luxor is accessible by a short aeroplane or overnight train. Known as the "World's Greatest Open-Air Museum," it's home to the Valley of the Kings, Karnak Temple, and Luxor Temple.

Ancient Tombs: Explore the ornate tombs of ancient pharaohs, including the famed tomb of Tutankhamun.

Aswan and Abu Simbel (Overnight Recommended):

Nubian Culture: Further south, Aswan gives a look into Nubian culture and picturesque views along the Nile. Highlights include the Philae Temple and the Unfinished Obelisk.

The Majestic Abu Simbel: A bit further from Aswan, the majestic temples of Abu Simbel, erected by Ramses II, are a tribute to ancient Egyptian magnificence and engineering brilliance.

These day trips from Cairo reveal the layers of history and culture that have defined Egypt. Each site offers a distinct story, immersing visitors in the mystery and majesty of ancient civilizations. Whether you're a history aficionado or a curious traveler, these excursions are sure to improve your Egyptian journey.

5.5 Desert Safaris Around Cairo

For those wanting adventure and a taste of the vast Egyptian wilderness, desert safaris surrounding Cairo are an amazing alternative. These safaris take you into the heart of the desert, delivering a blend of natural beauty, historical history, and thrilling adventures. Here's what you can expect from desert safari activities near Cairo

The Great Sahara Desert Experience:

Breathtaking vistas: Venture into the sweeping dunes and distinctive vistas of the Sahara, the largest scorching desert in the world.

Sunset and Sunrise Views: Witness the beautiful desert sunsets and sunrises, a pleasure for photographers and environment lovers alike.

Quad Biking and Dune Bashing:

Thrilling Rides For thrill junkies, quad riding and dune bashing in 4x4 vehicles offer an exciting way to negotiate the desert environment.

Guided Tours: These activities are generally part of guided tours, guaranteeing safety while giving an exhilarating experience.

Bedouin Culture and Overnight Camping:

Cultural Immersion Experience Bedouin hospitality, learn about their nomadic lifestyle, and enjoy traditional cuisine and music.

Stargazing: Desert nights offer some of the best stargazing possibilities, far from the light pollution of the city.

Visiting Ancient Sites:

Historical Excursions Some safaris include trips to lesser-known ancient sites and ruins located in the desert, presenting a distinct historical viewpoint.

Combining History and Adventure: This blend of adventure and history delivers a well-rounded experience of Egypt's many attractions.

Camel Treks:

Traditional Desert Travel For a more traditional experience, camel treks are available, allowing a slower, more introspective ride through the desert.

Scenic Routes: These treks generally follow scenic routes, providing for stunning views and a closer connection with the desert terrain.

Off-the-Beaten-Path Exploration:

Unique Locations Discover hidden valleys, secret oases, and unique geological formations that are off the main route.

Photographic chances: These sites provide fantastic chances for photography and witnessing the pristine beauty of the desert.

Safety and Preparation:

Expert Guides It's crucial to embark on these excursions with professional guides for safety and to get valuable knowledge about the desert.

Proper Gear: Ensure you have the necessary gear, including UV protection, appropriate clothing, and adequate hydration.

Desert safaris near Cairo offer a fascinating adventure, contrasting the hectic city life with the tranquil and enormous expanse of the desert. These adventures not only provide an adrenaline rush but also allow for a greater understanding of the natural beauty and historical history that Egypt has to offer. Whether it's a half-day excursion or an overnight adventure, a desert safari is an unforgettable aspect of the Egyptian experience.

Chapter 5

Family-Friendly Cairo

6.1 Kid-Friendly Attractions in Cairo

Cairo, with its rich history and vibrant culture, offers a plethora of family-friendly attractions that cater to both the young and the young at heart. Here are some kid-friendly activities and destinations to explore in Cairo:

Children's Civilization and Creativity Center (C4):

Educational Fun: C4 provides an interactive learning experience for children, combining education with creativity through various exhibits and workshops.

Hands-On Activities: Kids can engage in hands-on activities that stimulate their imagination and curiosity about science, art, and technology.

Giza Zoo:

Wildlife Adventure The Giza Zoo is a fantastic place for a family outing, featuring a diverse range of animals from around the world.

Animal Encounters: Children can enjoy close encounters with various species, making it an educational and entertaining day.

Dream Park:

Amusement Rides: Dream Park is an amusement park with a variety of rides suitable for different age groups, ensuring a day filled with excitement and laughter.

Entertainment Shows: The park often hosts entertaining shows and events for families to enjoy together.

Magic Galaxy:

Indoor Play Area Magic Galaxy is an indoor play center with a range of activities, including trampolines, climbing structures, and arcade games.

Safe Environment: It provides a safe and supervised environment for kids to play and socialize.

Cairo Opera House Children's Cultural Center:

Cultural Exploration The Children's Cultural Center at the Cairo Opera House offers cultural activities, performances, and workshops tailored for young audiences.

Artistic Expression: Kids can explore their artistic side through music, dance, and theater programs.

Heliopolis Model Library:

Storytime Sessions: The library in Heliopolis often organizes storytelling sessions and reading activities for children, fostering a love for literature.

Quiet Reading Spaces: It provides a calm environment for kids to discover the joy of reading.

Mall of Arabia Entertainment Zone:

Arcade and Games: The entertainment zone in Mall of Arabia features an arcade, games, and attractions suitable for children of various ages.

Ice Skating: Some areas include an ice skating rink, offering a cool and enjoyable experience for families.

Kidzania Cairo:

Role-Playing Adventures: Kidzania is an interactive city where children can role-play various professions, providing an educational and entertaining experience.

Real-Life Simulations: Kids get a taste of different careers in a simulated environment, combining learning with play.

Al-Azhar Park:

Green Spaces: Al-Azhar Park offers a tranquil retreat with gardens and open spaces, providing a relaxing environment for family picnics.

Playgrounds: There are playgrounds within the park where children can play while surrounded by the beauty of nature.

Aquarium Grotto Garden:

Underwater Exploration: This aquarium in Grotto Garden allows kids to explore underwater life and learn about marine ecosystems.

Interactive Exhibits: The exhibits are designed to be engaging and educational, making it an exciting journey for young marine enthusiasts.

Cairo's kid-friendly attractions offer a delightful blend of entertainment, education, and cultural exploration for families. Whether exploring the wonders of the animal kingdom, enjoying amusement park thrills, or engaging in creative activities, Cairo has something to captivate every child's imagination.

6.2 Educational Experiences for Children in Cairo

Cairo provides a choice of educational experiences for children, mixing learning with pleasure. Here are some engaging activities that contribute to the intellectual and cultural development of young minds:

Children's Civilization and Creativity Center (C4):

Interactive exhibitions: C4 offers fascinating exhibitions that span diverse aspects of science, technology, and art, stimulating curiosity and inquiry.

Workshops & Programs: The center organises workshops where children can participate in hands-on activities, boosting their learning experience.

The Children's Museum in Cairo:

Exploration Zones: This museum is designed to spark children's interest with interactive exhibits covering topics including history, geography, and science.

Learning through Play: Hands-on activities and play spaces allow kids to absorb knowledge in a lively and enjoyable atmosphere.

Planetarium Science Center:

Astronomy Education The Planetarium presents educational shows that teach children to the wonders of the universe, planets, and space exploration.

Hands-On Astronomy: Interactive exhibits and workshops provide a hands-on approach to learning about astronomy and scientific principles.

Bibliotheca Alexandrina Planetarium Science Center:

Stellar performances Located in Alexandria, this center presents planetarium performances that attract young audiences and spark an interest in astronomy.

Science Workshops: Workshops address numerous scientific topics, inviting youngsters to dig into the world of discovery.

Cairo Opera House Children's Cultural Center:

Artistic Workshops: The Cultural Center at the Cairo Opera House conducts artistic workshops and concerts especially for children.

Cultural Appreciation: Through music, dance, and theater, youngsters learn an awareness and appreciation of various cultural manifestations.

Egyptian Museum of Antiquities:

Historical Exploration While mostly known for its ancient treasures, the museum offers educational programs that transport children to Egypt's rich historical past.

Archaeological Adventures: Special tours and activities are meant to make history come alive for young learners.

Science Fun:

Mobile Science laboratories: Some groups operate mobile science laboratories that tour schools and communities, delivering interactive science experiments for youngsters.

Hands-On Science: These seminars attempt to make science pleasant and accessible, inspiring a love for exploration and discovery.

Educational Workshops at Libraries:

Literary Adventures Public libraries typically arrange educational activities, including storytelling sessions and book clubs, fostering literacy and a love for reading.

Language Development: Workshops may focus on language skills, enabling children to express themselves via writing and communication.

Art Studios for Kids:

Creative Expression Various art studios in Cairo provide programmes specifically targeted for youngsters, letting them explore their artistic talents.

Crafting and Design: Kids can engage in activities like painting, drawing, and crafting, developing creativity and self-expression.

STEM Programs:

Robotics and Coding Classes: Some educational facilities provide STEM (Science, Technology, Engineering, and Mathematics) programs, introducing youngsters to the principles of robotics and coding.

Innovative Learning: These programs emphasize problem-solving and innovation, preparing pupils for the technological challenges of the future.

Cairo's educational experiences for children go beyond traditional learning, supporting a holistic approach that combines science, arts, culture, and exploration. These activities attempt to create a love for learning and curiosity that will benefit youngsters throughout their life.

6.3 Parks and Recreation Areas in Cairo

Cairo offers a variety of parks and leisure spaces where locals and visitors alike may escape the hustle and bustle of the city, relax, and enjoy outdoor sports. Here are some noteworthy parks and green spots in Cairo:

Al-Azhar Park:

Lush Gardens Al-Azhar Park is a magnificently planted green park in the heart of historic Cairo, boasting gardens with fountains and stunning views of Islamic Cairo's cityscape.

Cultural Venue: Apart from greenery, the park hosts cultural events and features a restaurant where guests may enjoy both nature and Egyptian food.

Al-Azhar Park Lakeside:

Serene Lakeside Setting Adjacent to Al-Azhar Park, this lakeside area offers a tranquil environment with shaded sitting, providing an ideal site for relaxation.

picturesque Views: Visitors can enjoy picturesque views of the park's lake and surrounding flora.

Al-Montazah Park:

Situated along the Mediterranean, Al-Montazah Park offers a refreshing coastal hideaway with spacious grass and sea vistas.

Palatial Gardens: The garden surrounds the Montaza Palace, lending a touch of regal beauty to its environment.

Orman Botanical Garden:

Botanical Diversity: Established in 1875, Orman Botanical Garden is a wide expanse of greenery with a diverse assortment of plants and trees.

Educational Opportunities: The garden acts as an educational resource, allowing visitors to learn about numerous plant species.

Al-Azhar Park Family Area:

Family-Friendly Atmosphere This designated family area within Al-Azhar Park provides a safe and fun location for children and their families.

Playgrounds and Activities: Kids can engage in play activities, and families can have picnics in a nice atmosphere.

Family Park, Maadi:

Recreational Facilities: This park in the Maadi area includes recreational facilities such as playgrounds, making it a great destination for families.

Open Spaces: The park's open spaces provide a comfortable location for picnics and outdoor meetings.

Al Horreya Garden:

Historic Gardens: Located in Zamalek, Al Horreya Garden is noted for its historical significance and tranquil ambiance.

Relaxation Spot: Visitors can unwind in a serene location surrounded by trees and well-maintained flora.

Giza Zoo:

Zoological Park While essentially a zoo, Giza Zoo also has wide green spaces where tourists can take leisurely strolls.

Animal Encounters: Families can enjoy a day touring the zoo and its wide assortment of animals.

El Nahda Park:

Community Gathering El Nahda Park in Heliopolis is a popular area for folks to meet, relax, and enjoy outdoor activities.

Sports Facilities: The park includes sports facilities, including courts for basketball and tennis.

Cairo Festival City Mall's Central Park:

Urban respite This centrally placed park within Cairo Festival City Mall gives a green respite amid the urban atmosphere.

Retail and relaxation: Visitors can mix shopping with relaxation, enjoying the park's environment.

These parks appeal to varied desires, whether one seeks a calm getaway, a family-friendly atmosphere, or recreational activities. Cairo's green spaces contribute to the well-being of its citizens, establishing a balance between the city's bustle and the quiet of nature

6.4 Family-Friendly Dining and Accommodations in Cairo

Cairo welcomes families with a selection of dining options and accommodations that cater to the different needs of parents and children. Whether you're looking for kid-friendly cuisine or roomy hotels, Cairo provides something for every family.

Here are some recommendations:

Family-Friendly Dining:

Andrea El Mariouteya:

Culinary Variety: This family-friendly restaurant offers a broad menu with Egyptian and international foods, appealing to various preferences.

Outdoor Seating: Families can enjoy their meals in a beautiful outdoor setting.

Crave Restaurant:

Kid-Friendly Menu: Crave features a specific kids' menu with a selection of foods that appeal to younger tastes.

comfortable Ambiance: The restaurant's comfortable setting makes it excellent for family meals.

Zooba Eats:

Egyptian Street Food: Zooba Eats delivers a unique experience with its modern interpretation on traditional Egyptian street food.

Casual Setting: Families can enjoy a casual dining environment while sampling local flavors.

Kazouza:

Child-Friendly Atmosphere: Kazouza is known for its casual setting, making it appropriate for families with children.

Fresh Juices: The restaurant offers a range of fresh juices, suitable for a family outing.

Lucille's:

world Cuisine: Lucille's serves a blend of world cuisines, allowing options for various gastronomic preferences within the family.

nice Décor: Families can dine in a nice setting with a welcoming attitude.

Family-Friendly Accommodations:

Fairmont Nile City Luxury Stay: This hotel offers a magnificent experience with family-friendly features, including spacious rooms and an outdoor pool.

Convenient Location: Located along the Nile, it provides convenient access to popular sights.

Conrad Cairo:

Nile Views Conrad Cairo features Nile River views and family-friendly amenities, offering a relaxing stay for all.

Recreational Facilities: The hotel includes facilities like a pool and fitness center for family enjoyment.

InterContinental Cairo Citystars:

Connected to Citystars Mall: Ideal for families, this hotel is connected to Citystars Mall, allowing easy access to shopping and entertainment.

Family Suites: Spacious family suites are available for enhanced comfort.

Kempinski Nile Hotel:

Rooftop Pool Families can enjoy the rooftop pool with breathtaking views of the Nile.

excellent Dining: The hotel offers excellent dining options for a special family supper.

Dusit Thani LakeView Cairo:

Garden Setting Set in a lush garden area, our hotel provides a tranquil atmosphere for families.

Kids Club: The Kids Club offers activities for children, offering a delightful visit for the whole family.

Royal Maxim Palace Kempinski Cairo:

Elegant Stay: Families may experience elegance and luxury at this palace-style hotel.

Landscaped grounds: The hotel's landscaped grounds offer a pleasant escape for families.

Le Méridien Cairo Airport:

Airport Convenience: Ideal for families on the go, this hotel gives handy access to Cairo International Airport.

Family-Friendly Services: Offers family rooms and amenities for a comfortable stay.

These dining and housing alternatives aim to enhance the family experience in Cairo, giving both comfort and delight for parents and children alike.

Chapter 6

Practical Information

7.1 Transportation: Getting Around Cairo

Navigating Cairo, one of the most populous cities in Africa, can be a fascinating yet tough experience. The city offers many transportation alternatives tailored for diverse interests and purposes. Here's a guide to help you understand and utilize Cairo's transit system:

Metro:

Efficient and Cost-Effective Cairo's metro is one of the fastest ways to travel around, avoiding the notorious traffic bottlenecks.

Extensive Network: It spans numerous regions of the city, including key attractions and districts.

Regular Service: Trains run at frequent intervals, especially during peak hours.

Affordable: Metro tickets are very affordable compared to other types of transportation.

Taxis:

Convenient: Taxis are widely available around Cairo.

Metered Fares: Ensure that the meter is running to avoid being overcharged. Some taxis may not utilise meters, so discuss the fare ahead.

Ride-Hailing Apps: Services like Uber and Careem are functioning in Cairo, giving a safer and more reliable alternative to traditional taxis.

Buses and Mini-Buses:

Extensive Coverage: Buses and mini-buses cover a larger area of Cairo.

Economical: They are cheaper than cabs but can be packed.

Learning Routes: It might be tough for novices to comprehend routes and stops, as there is limited signage in English.

Car Rentals:

Flexibility: Renting a car allows the freedom to explore at your own speed.

Driving Conditions Be prepared for Cairo's heavy traffic and various driving styles.

Parking: Finding parking might be tough in crowded places.

Bicycles:

Eco-Friendly: Some regions of Cairo are researching bike-friendly pathways.

Limited Scope: Cycling is not commonly used due to traffic and safety issues.

Walking:

Feasible in Certain districts: Walking is a decent alternative in pedestrian-friendly districts including Downtown, Zamalek, and some portions of Old Cairo.

Be Cautious: Always be careful of vehicles, as pedestrian crossings and walkways may be limited.

Nile River Boats:

Scenic and Pleasant: For a new perspective of Cairo, consider taking a boat ride on the Nile.

Limited Practical Use: While it's a unique experience, it's not the most effective method to travel for regular commutes.

Rickshaws:

Common in Suburbs: Mainly found in the suburbs and residential regions.

Short Distances: Suitable for short distances inside local neighborhoods.

Horse-Drawn Carriages:

Tourist Attraction: Mostly found surrounding tourist destinations like the Pyramids.

Negotiate Fares: Ensure you agree on a price before commencing your journey.

Each form of transit in Cairo has its own set of advantages and challenges. It's advisable to choose based on your destination, money, time of day, and personal comfort. For tourists, a combination of the metro, taxis (particularly ride-hailing apps), and occasional walking often gives a balanced and effective method to experience the city.

7.2 Accommodation: From Budget to Luxury

Cairo, a city with a rich history and dynamic culture, offers a broad choice of lodging alternatives to suit all interests and budgets. Whether you're seeking for a deluxe accommodation or a budget-friendly choice, Cairo has something for everyone. Here's a resource to help you discover the best spot to stay during your visit:

Luxury Hotels:

Premier Experience: Cairo features several five-star hotels noted for their superb service, exquisite rooms, and luxury amenities.

Notable Names: Brands like the Four Seasons, The Ritz-Carlton, and Kempinski have properties in great sites, affording spectacular views of the Nile or the Pyramids.

Facilities: Expect world-class spas, exquisite restaurants, and state-of-the-art exercise centers.

Boutique Hotels:

Unique Charm For a more customised experience, boutique hotels in Cairo provide distinct character and typically reflect Egyptian tradition in their decor.

Locations: Many are located in historic or culturally significant regions, like Zamalek or near Islamic Cairo.

Service: These hotels often give attentive, individualized service.

Mid-Range Hotels:

Balanced Option These hotels offer a comfortable stay without the high price tag of luxury hotels.

facilities: Expect clean rooms, basic facilities, and possibly an in-house restaurant or swimming pool.

Chain Hotels: International brands including Novotel, Hilton Garden Inn, and Holiday Inn are present, alongside local options.

Budget Accommodations:

Hostels and Guesthouses Ideal for backpackers and lone travelers, hostels in Cairo give economical lodging with options for private or communal rooms.

Basic Amenities: These motels offer the essentials, generally including free Wi-Fi, communal facilities, and sometimes a small breakfast.

Locations: Concentrated in regions like Downtown Cairo, adjacent to main attractions and public transit.

Serviced Apartments:

Home Away from Home Perfect for longer visits or for individuals who prefer a more homely environment.

Facilities: These apartments come with kitchenettes, laundry facilities, and sometimes include housekeeping services.

Variety: Ranging from inexpensive to luxury, they may accommodate lone travelers, couples, or families.

Airbnb and Vacation Rentals:

Local Experience: Renting flats or rooms through platforms like Airbnb might give a more authentic experience in Cairo.

Diverse Options: From modern flats in New Cairo to classic residences in older areas, there's a vast choice to choose from.

freedom: These rentals frequently provide greater freedom and privacy than hotels.

Nile River Cruises:

Unique Accommodation: Some cruises provide overnight stays, combining accommodation with a gorgeous ride along the Nile.

Inclusive Packages: These frequently include meals and guided tours to historical locations.

When picking accommodation in Cairo, consider aspects like location, closeness to activities, transit choices, and your particular travel style. It's also advisable to read reviews and check for recent traveler experiences, especially for budget and mid-range options, to assure quality and safety. Whether going for the splendour of a luxury hotel or the simplicity of a hostel,

Cairo's range of lodgings is sure to enrich your stay in this timeless city.

7.3 Health and Safety Tips

Ensuring a safe and healthy experience during your visit to Cairo is vital. Here are key health and safety tips to bear in mind while touring this dynamic city:

Stay Hydrated:

Environment Awareness Cairo has a desert environment, and temperatures can be high, especially in the summer. Stay hydrated by drinking plenty of water throughout the day.

Bottled Water: Opt for bottled water to assure its purity.

Protect Against the Sun:

Sunscreen Apply sunscreen with a high SPF to protect your skin from the fierce Egyptian sun.

Appropriate Clothing: Wear lightweight, long-sleeved clothing and a cap to shelter yourself from the sun.

Food and Water Safety:

Avoid Tap Water Stick to bottled or purified water and avoid drinking tap water.

Street Food Caution: While street food is appealing, seek vendors with high foot traffic to decrease the danger of contaminated infections.

Traffic and Pedestrian Safety:

Crossing Streets Exercise caution when crossing roads. Follow local pedestrians and use marked crosswalks.

Traffic Flow: Be aware of the local traffic patterns, and exhibit patience when navigating crowded streets.

Health Precautions:

immunisations Ensure routine immunisations are up-to-date. Depending on your travel history, consider extra immunisations like Hepatitis A and Typhoid.

Medical Kit: Pack a basic medical kit with essentials including pain painkillers, stomach pills, and any necessary prescription drugs.

COVID-19 Considerations:

Check Guidelines Stay informed about the newest COVID-19 guidelines and rules released by local authorities.

Mask Usage: Adhere to mask-wearing requirements, especially in crowded or indoor areas.

Vaccination: Consider getting immunised against COVID-19 before traveling.

Emergency Services:

Know Emergency Numbers Familiarize yourself with local emergency numbers for police, medical services, and your country's embassy or consulate.

Travel Insurance: Have comprehensive travel insurance that covers medical crises and evacuation if needed.

Cultural Sensitivity:

observe Local Customs: Be mindful of and observe local customs, particularly in holy sites. Dress modestly when visiting mosques or churches.

Photography Etiquette: Ask for permission before photographing individuals, especially in more conservative locations.

Currency and Valuables:

Secure Belongings Keep your belongings secure to prevent theft. Use a money belt or lockable bag for critical documents and valuables.

currencies Exchange: Be cautious while exchanging currencies and choose reputed providers.

Local Laws and Regulations:

Stay Informed: Familiarise oneself with local rules and regulations. This involves understanding the legal drinking age and respecting local norms.

Medical Facilities:

Know Nearby Hospitals: Identify the locations of hospitals or medical clinics in the places you want to visit.

Emergency Assistance: In case of a medical emergency, contact your embassy or consulate for assistance.

By remaining educated, respecting local customs, and taking appropriate care, you may contribute to a safe and pleasurable stay in Cairo. Flexibility and cultural awareness are vital, allowing you to make the most of your time in this lively and historically rich city.

7.4 Cultural Etiquette and Customs

Respecting cultural etiquette is vital for a happy and harmonious stay in Cairo. Here are some basic suggestions to negotiate the local customs with respect and understanding:

Greetings:

Handshakes are popular between people of the same gender. Men may also exchange cheek kisses, although it's recommended to wait for your local counterpart to do this.

Clothing:

Modesty in Religious Sites: When visiting mosques or churches, both men and women should dress modestly. Women may need to cover their heads in specific religious venues.

Casual dress: In ordinary contexts, casual dress is often appropriate. However, modesty is prized, especially in more conservative areas.

Respect for Religion:

Mosque Etiquette Remove your shoes before entering a mosque. Non-Muslims are normally not allowed in particular portions of mosques, therefore respect the specified places.

Christian Sites: Similar to mosques, assume a courteous manner when visiting Christian churches.

Public Behavior:

Affection in Public Public shows of affection should be maintained to a minimum, as excessive displays may be regarded improper.

Respect for seniors: Show respect to seniors, and use courteous language while engaging with elderly folks.

Dining Etiquette:

Accepting Hospitality If invited to someone's home, it's traditional to accept with appreciation. Remove your shoes before entering, and express appreciation for the hospitality.

Eating with Right Hand: When dining, it's typical to eat with the right hand, as the left hand is generally considered less clean.

Language Considerations:

Arabic Greetings Learning a few Arabic greetings is welcomed and demonstrates a genuine interest in the local culture.

English Usage: English is generally understood, especially in tourist regions, however making an attempt to speak a few Arabic phrases is viewed as respectable.

Photography Courtesy:

Ask Permission Always ask for permission before snapping images of people, particularly in more conservative or private circumstances.

Sensitive Locations: Avoid snapping images in sensitive areas, such as military sites or certain government buildings.

Bargaining:

Market Etiquette: Bargaining is typical in marketplaces. Approach it with a friendly approach, and be prepared to bargain in good spirits.

Social Invitations:

Accepting Invitations: If invited to a social gathering, it's polite to accept, even if it's just for a short period. Expressing thanks is crucial.

Friday Observance:

Friday Prayer Friday is a holy day, and the midday Friday prayer is significant. Certain businesses and services may close at this time.

Currency Handling:

Respect for Currency Treat the local currency and pictures of leaders with respect. Avoid treading on or mishandling money.

Tipping Etiquette:

Service Gratuity: Tipping is typical at restaurants and for various services. It's a show of thanks for good service.

By embracing these cultural etiquette tips, you'll not only show respect for the local customs but also enrich your cultural immersion in Cairo. Being open-minded and adaptable will contribute to a more meaningful and pleasurable experience in this bustling city.

7.5 Weather and Best Times to Visit

Understanding the environment and picking the perfect time to visit Cairo can drastically affect your trip. Here's a guide to the weather and the ideal times to tour the city:

Environment Overview: Cairo faces a hot desert environment with high temperatures and low precipitation. There are two main seasons: a hot summer and a moderate winter.

Summer (May to September):
Temperature High temperatures might surpass 40°C (104°F).
Sun Exposure: Intense sunshine, making outdoor activities problematic during peak hours.
Tourist Traffic: Some passengers may find the heat uncomfortable, resulting in fewer tourists.

Winter (October to April):
Temperature: Cooler temperatures range from mild to warm, with daily highs averaging from 18°C to 24°C (64°F to 75°F).

Comfortable Conditions: Winter is considered the ideal time to come due to milder weather.

Tourist Peak: The period from October to April is the main tourist season.

Best Times to Visit:

Fall (October to November):

Temperature Pleasant weather with cooler temps.

Cultural Festivals: Cairo hosts cultural activities and festivals during this time.

Sightseeing: Ideal for viewing historical places without the strong summer heat.

Spring (March to April):

Temperature: Mild temperatures make outdoor activities enjoyable.

Floral Blooms: Spring offers some greenery and flowering flowers.

Historical Exploration: Comfortable weather for exploring sights.

Winter (December to February):

Temperature: Cooler but generally acceptable temps.

Peak Tourist Season: This is the high tourist season; expect more tourists.

Festive Atmosphere: Festivals and activities may take place.

Weather Considerations:

Sun Protection:

Sunscreen Regardless of the season, wear sunscreen to protect against harsh sunlight.

Hydration: Carry water to stay hydrated, especially during the hot summer.

Clothing:

Light Clothing In summer, wear light, breathable clothing.

Layers: In winter, layering is advisable for variable temperatures.

Special Events:

Ramadan: If visiting during Ramadan, be conscious of cultural rituals and the impact on dining and daily routines.

Tourist Volume:

Plan Ahead During high visitor seasons, popular sights may be busier, so plan accordingly.

Off-Peak Exploration: Visiting during shoulder seasons provides for a more relaxing experience.

Understanding Cairo's weather trends and planning your vacation appropriately will help to a more enjoyable and comfortable stay in this bustling city. Whether you prefer the cooler temps of fall and spring or are fine with the warmth of summer, Cairo provides unique activities year-round.

Chapter 7

Planning Your Trip

8.1 Possible Itineraries

The city of Cairo has a lot to offer in terms of history, culture, and attractions, so making a plan for your trip there might be exciting. Depending on your interests and the length of your trip, here are some possible itineraries:

Cultural and Historical Pursuers: A One-Day Programme

Morning Visit the renowned Pyramids of Giza and the Sphinx. Get there before the masses.

The afternoon is a great time to visit the Egyptian Museum and see the priceless treasures of Tutankhamun and other ancient Egyptians.

In the evening, take a leisurely stroll through Islamic Cairo, seeing its ancient mosques and bustling Khan El Khalili market.

Our 3-Day Programme:

Day 1: Follow the 1-day itinerary.

Day 2: Morning: Tour Coptic Cairo, including the Hanging Church and the Coptic Museum.

Afternoon: Stop at the Muhammad Ali Mosque and the Saladin Citadel.

Evening: Enjoy a Nile river dinner cruise with traditional entertainment.

Third Day: First Thing in the Morning: Saqqara and the Step Pyramid.

Afternoon: Visit the Dahshur pyramids.

Evening: Experience cultural entertainment or a typical Egyptian supper.

For Families 1-Day Itinerary:

Morning: Visit the Giza Zoo and Orman Botanical Garden.

Afternoon: Explore the Pharaonic Village for an interactive ancient Egypt adventure.

Evening: Relax at Al-Azhar Park and enjoy the views of the city.

Our 3-Day Programme:

Day 1: Follow the 1-day itinerary.

Day 2: Morning: Visit the Aquarium Grotto Garden.

Afternoon: Head to KidZania Cairo for educational and amusing activities for youngsters.

Evening: Dine in a family-friendly restaurant with traditional Egyptian cuisine.

Day 3: Morning: Take a felucca trip on the Nile.

Afternoon: Visit the Cairo Tower for panoramic city views.

Evening: Explore the interactive displays at the Children's Civilization and Creativity Center.

For Adventure Seekers 1-Day Itinerary:

Morning: Experience a hot air balloon flight above Cairo.

Afternoon: Go on a desert safari in the adjacent Sahara Desert.

Evening: Try the traditional Egyptian street food at nearby marketplaces.

Our 3-Day Programme:

Day 1: Follow the 1-day itinerary.

Day 2: Morning: Camel or horseback tour around the Giza plateau.

Afternoon: Explore the lesser-known Red Pyramid and Bent Pyramid at Dahshur.

Evening: Enjoy a colourful evening in the busy area of Zamalek.

Day 3: Morning: Day trip to Alexandria or a neighbouring historic site.

Afternoon: Relax at a classic Egyptian hammam (bathhouse).

Evening: Discover Cairo's nightlife, including clubs and late-night cafes.

For Art and Lifestyle Enthusiasts 1-Day Itinerary:

Morning: Visit the Museum of Modern Egyptian Art.

Afternoon: Explore modern art galleries in Zamalek.

Evening: Attend a performance at the Cairo Opera House or an art event.

Our 3-Day Programme:

Day 1: Follow the 1-day itinerary.

Day 2: Morning: Visit the Townhouse Gallery and other art locations in downtown Cairo.

Afternoon: Explore the rich street art in places like Coptic Cairo.

Evening: Enjoy food and entertainment in the fashionable area of Maadi.

Day 3: Morning: Wander through the El Sawy Culturewheel for various cultural events.

Afternoon: Visit the Darb 1718 Contemporary Art and Culture Center.

Evening: Explore Cairo's food scene, ranging from traditional eateries to sophisticated establishments.

These itineraries give a healthy mix of sightseeing, cultural immersion, and relaxation, customised to different types of travelers and durations of stay. They can be altered based on personal interests, pace, and preferences.

8.2 Booking Tours and Experiences

When planning your visit to Cairo, reserving tours and experiences in advance can enhance your trip, ensuring you have access to the greatest guides and chances. Here's a guide on how to book tours and experiences efficiently:

Online Booking Platforms

Specialized Travel Websites: Websites like Viator, GetYourGuide, and Tripadvisor offer a wide choice of excursions and activities in Cairo. These platforms include user reviews, which can help in making informed choices.

Local travel Operators: Many local Egyptian travel operators have internet booking possibilities. They frequently offer unique local experiences and can provide more personalized service.

Travel agency: Traditional travel agency can also arrange trips and experiences as part of a broader travel package.

What to Look for in a Tour

Reviews and Ratings: Check the reviews and ratings of the tour to judge the quality and reliability.

Group Size: Consider if you prefer a private tour or feel comfortable in a larger group environment.

Guide Credentials: Ensure that the guides are knowledgeable and licensed, especially for historical and cultural trips.

Inclusions and Exclusions: Check what the tour price includes (e.g., admission fees, transportation, lunches) and what is extra.

Types of Tours and Experiences

Cultural and Historical Tours: These include guided tours of the Pyramids, Islamic Cairo, Coptic Cairo, and museums.

Adventure trips: Options including desert safaris, camel rides, and Nile felucca trips.

Food and Culinary excursions: Guided excursions to explore Egyptian cuisine, including street food tours and culinary classes.

Art and Lifestyle Tours: These focus on Cairo's modern art scene, local markets, and neighborhoods.

Custom and Private Tours

Tailored Experiences: Some operators provide personalised tours where you can determine your itinerary.

Personal Guides: Private excursions with personal guides provide a more intimate and flexible experience.

Booking Tips

Book in Advance: Especially for popular monuments like the Giza Pyramids, reserving in advance is vital to avoid disappointment.

Check for Cancellation Policies: Look for trips with flexible cancellation policies in case your plans change.

Payment and Confirmation: Ensure secure payment methods and acquire a confirmation with information of the excursion.

Local Experiences

Workshops and lessons: Engage in local arts and crafts workshops or cooking lessons for a hands-on experience.

Community Tours: Some excursions focus on local towns and lifestyle, delivering a greater cultural immersion.

Contacting the Provider

If you have unique requests or questions, don't hesitate to contact the tour provider directly before booking. They may often fulfil specific requests or provide additional information. By considering these aspects and planning ahead, you can guarantee that your trips and experiences in Cairo are enjoyable, safe, and well-suited to your interests.

8.3 Language Tips: Basic Arabic for Travelers

While English is widely understood in Cairo, learning some basic Arabic phrases can greatly enhance your travel experience and show respect for the local culture. Here are essential Arabic phrases for travelers:

Greetings:

Hello: As-salamu alaykum (السلام عليكم)

Reply to Hello: Wa alaykumu as-salam (وعليكم السلام)

Good morning: Sabah al-khayr (صباح الخير)

Good evening: Masa' al-khayr (مساء الخير)

Courtesy Phrases:

Please: Min fadlak (من فضلك)

Thank you: Shukran (شكرا)

You're welcome: Afwan (عفوا)

Excuse me / I'm sorry: Asif (آسف)

Basic Questions:

Yes: Na'am (نعم)

No: La (لا)

Where is...?: Ayna...? (أين...؟)

How much is this?: Kam hatha? (كم هذا؟)

What is this?: Ma hatha? (ما هذا؟)

Getting Around:

I want a taxi: Ureed taxi (أريد تاكسي)

Where is the hotel?: Ayna al-funduq? (أين الفندق؟)

Airport: Mataar (مطار)

Train station: Mahatta al-qitar (محطة القطار)

Eating Out:

Menu: Al-Qa'ima (القائمة)

Water: Ma'a (ماء)

I don't eat...: Ana la akol... (أنا لا أكل...)

Numbers:

1: Wahed (واحد)

2: Itnan (اثنان)

3: Talata (ثلاثة)

10: Ashara (عشرة)

Emergencies:

Help: Musa'ada (مساعدة)

Doctor: Tabib (طبيب)

Police: Shurta (شرطة)

I need assistance: Ureed musa'ada (أريد مساعدة)

Learning and using these basic Arabic phrases will not only make your interactions smoother but also convey your appreciation for the local culture. Egyptians are generally appreciative when visitors make an effort to speak their language.

8.4 Money Matters: Currency, Tipping, and Bargaining

Understanding the currency, tipping etiquette, and negotiation procedures in Cairo will increase your financial transactions and cultural connections. Here's a guide on money matters in the city:

Currency:

Currency: The official currency is the Egyptian Pound (EGP). It's wise to have some local cash for little transactions and markets.

ATMs: ATMs are extensively available in Cairo. They accept major international credit and debit cards. Check with your bank for overseas transaction fees.

Currency Exchange: Exchange currency at banks, authorized exchange offices, or your hotel. Avoid unlicensed street vendors for currency exchange.

Tipping: Service Charge: Some restaurants and motels incorporate a service charge. If not, a 10% tip is usual.

Tour Guides: It's normal to tip tour guides. A tip of roughly 10-15% of the tour cost is appreciated.

Taxis: Tipping taxi drivers is not necessary, but rounding up the fare is usual.

Porters: If someone helps with your luggage, a tip of a few Egyptian Pounds is usual.

Bargaining: Markets and Bazaars: Bargaining is typical in markets. Start by offering half the initial price and negotiate from there. Be friendly and respectful.

Politeness is Key: Maintain a warm demeanor during bargaining. If the vendor doesn't agree on a price, be prepared to walk away.

Know the Value: Have a general sense of the item's value before haggling. Local vendors welcome knowledgeable shoppers.

General Tips: Cash is King: While cards are accepted in many locations, cash is preferred, especially in smaller shops and marketplaces.

Check Your Change: Count your change carefully, especially in cabs and tiny shops.

Small Denominations: Keep small denominations for tips and modest purchases.

Negotiate with Respect: Bargaining is a cultural norm, but it's crucial to negotiate properly without undervaluing the seller's goods.

Understanding these areas of money matters in Cairo will assist to a smoother and more enjoyable experience throughout your visit.

Chapter 8

Beyond Cairo

9.1 Exploring the Nile Delta

The Nile Delta, a fertile and culturally rich region in the north of Egypt, gives a unique chance for exploration. Here's a guide to make the most of your visit to this beautiful area:

Geography and Importance: Formation: The Delta is formed as the Nile River extends out and flows into the Mediterranean Sea. It's one of the world's largest river deltas.

Agricultural Heartland: Known as Egypt's breadbasket, the Delta is essential for the country's agriculture, providing rich land for cultivating commodities.

Key Destinations:

Alexandria: A historic port city with a blend of Greco-Roman and Egyptian heritage. Must-visits include the Bibliotheca Alexandrina, the Catacombs, and the Citadel of Qaitbay.

Rosetta (Rashid): Famous for the Rosetta Stone, it provides great architectural heritage with its Ottoman-style mansions.

Tanta: Known for its huge mosque and the yearly Moulid of Sayid Ahmed el-Badawi event, bringing millions of people.

Cultural Experiences: Cuisine: Sample traditional meals that may differ from those in other places of Egypt. The Delta region is famed for its fresh fish and seafood.

Village Life: Experience the rural way of life in one of the many communities. Agriculture is a way of life here, and the pace is slower than in Cairo.

Nature and Wildlife: Bird Watching: The Delta is a refuge for bird watchers, especially during migratory seasons.

Lush Landscapes: Explore the verdant, rich lands, a sharp contrast to Egypt's deserts.

Historical Sites:

Ancient Ruins: There are several archaeological sites dispersed around the Delta, although less frequented than those in other parts of Egypt.

Tips for Visiting:

Travel Arrangements: Consider hiring a local guide or taking a tour for a more informed experience.

Accommodation: Stay in a selection of accommodations from small guesthouses to more opulent alternatives in bigger towns like Alexandria.

Local Interaction: Engage with the locals to learn more about the Delta's culture and traditions.

Transportation: The Delta is well-connected by road and rail, making it convenient to explore different places.

Exploring the Nile Delta offers a view into a less-traveled portion of Egypt, full with rich history, unique cultures, and magnificent landscapes. It's a voyage that contrasts the desert and ancient monumental experiences of the rest of Egypt.

9.2 Adventures on the Sinai Peninsula

The Sinai Peninsula, a place of diverse landscapes and historical significance, invites adventure seekers. Here's your guide to embarking on adventurous experiences in this interesting region:

Geographic Wonders: Mount Sinai (Jebel Musa): Ascend this legendary mountain to enjoy a beautiful dawn. It carries religious importance and offers panoramic views of the surrounding desert.

Colored Canyon: Explore the brilliant hues of the Colored Canyon, a natural marvel with small tunnels and high, multicolored walls.

beach Bliss: Dahab: A laid-back beach town with a dynamic atmosphere. Enjoy aquatic sports include snorkeling, diving in the Blue Hole, and windsurfing.

Ras Mohamed National Park: Discover rich marine life in the Red Sea. Snorkel or dive in this protected region noted for its coral reefs.

Cultural Encounters: St. Catherine's Monastery: Visit one of the oldest continually operating Christian monasteries. The Burning Bush and old writings are noteworthy.

Bedouin Experiences: Engage with local Bedouin communities for a real cultural experience. Experience their friendliness and traditions.

Desert Expeditions: White Canyon: Trek through the strange terrain of the White Canyon, famed for its chalky white rock formations.

Sandboarding at Al-Fayoum Oasis: Try sandboarding on the dunes of Al-Fayoum for an adrenaline-packed adventure.

Under the Stars: Stargazing in the Desert: The Sinai night sky is captivating. Consider a stargazing expedition for an awe-inspiring celestial experience.

Practical Tips:

Guided Tours: Opt for guided tours, especially for activities like mountain treks, to ensure safety and good navigation.

Camping: Experience the splendour of the desert by camping under the stars. Several organized campsites offer a distinctive Bedouin-style experience.

Local Cuisine: taste traditional Bedouin cuisine and regional delicacies, adding a gourmet adventure to your Sinai vacation.

Safety Considerations:

Travel Alerts: Stay informed on the current situation and travel advice for the Sinai Peninsula.

Local Advice: Consult with local guides or officials for updated information on safe sites and activities.

Environmental Awareness:

Responsible Tourism: Respect the vulnerable desert ecology. Follow Leave No Trace principles and support eco-friendly projects.

The Sinai Peninsula encourages intrepid travelers to explore its various landscapes, from towering mountains to beautiful coral reefs. Whether seeking cultural exchanges, desert escapades, or aquatic wonders, the Sinai guarantees an unforgettable trip off the main route.

9.3 Discovering Alexandria: The Mediterranean Jewel

Alexandria, dubbed as the "Pearl of the Mediterranean," is a city steeped in history and culture. Once the heart of ancient civilization, today it is a bustling metropolis that integrates its historical history with modern living. Here's a guide to exploring this wonderful Egyptian city

Historical Landmarks: The Bibliotheca Alexandrina: A modern monument to the ancient Library of Alexandria, this architectural marvel is a nexus of knowledge, art, and history.

The Citadel of Qaitbay: Built on the site of the historic Lighthouse of Alexandria, one of the Seven Wonders of the historic World, this 15th-century fortress gives stunning sea vistas and a peek into Alexandria's military past.

Pompey's Pillar: A Roman triumphal column, it stands as a witness to the Roman presence in Egypt.

Roman Amphitheatre: Discover the well-preserved ruins of this ancient monument, affording insight into the recreational life of Roman-era Alexandrians.

Cultural Experiences: Alexandria National Museum: Journey through Egypt's history, from the Pharaonic era to present times, with relics and displays housed in an Italian-style palace.

Stanley Bridge: A modern icon, great for a picturesque walk and photo opportunity, especially around sunset.

Montaza Palace and Gardens: Explore the royal gardens and palaces, showing a blend of Ottoman and Florentine architectural styles.

Culinary Delights:

Seafood Galore: Being a coastal city, Alexandria is known for its fresh and excellent seafood. Enjoy meals at local eateries along the Corniche.

classic Cafés: Experience the city's age-old coffee culture at its classic cafés, where intellectuals and artists commonly gather.

Beachside Bliss: Mediterranean Beaches: Relax on Alexandria's beautiful beaches or enjoy water activities. Popular beaches include Maamoura and Montazah Beach.

Corniche Walk: Stroll along the Corniche, a waterfront promenade, for breathtaking views and a flavour of local life.

Shopping and Leisure: Souk Districts: Explore historic markets and souks for unique handicrafts, spices, and souvenirs.

Modern Shopping: For a contemporary shopping experience, visit the city's modern malls and boutiques.

Around Alexandria: El Alamein: A short drive away, this town is famous for its WWII cemeteries and museums.

Mediterranean Cruises: Alexandria acts as a gateway for Mediterranean cruises, allowing opportunity to explore various coastal destinations.

Practical Tips:

Transportation: Utilize taxis or the tram system for convenient city travel.

Best Time to Visit: Spring (March to May) and autumn (September to November) offer nice weather, great for visiting the city.

Language: While Arabic is the primary language, English and French are frequently spoken in tourist regions.

Cultural Etiquette:

Respectful Attire: Dress modestly, especially while visiting religious or traditional locations.

Cultural Sensitivity: Be observant of local customs and traditions, particularly during religious festivals.

Alexandria, with its rich history, cultural depth, and Mediterranean appeal, offers a distinct experience compared to the rest of Egypt. Whether it's discovering ancient ruins, enjoying the sea breeze, or delving into the local culinary scene, Alexandria guarantees a remarkable trip through time and culture.

9.4 Luxor and Aswan: Gateways to Ancient Egypt

Venture beyond Cairo and immerse yourself in the timeless beauties of Luxor and Aswan, two cities on the banks of the majestic Nile River. Here's a guide to uncovering the mysteries and marvels of ancient Egypt in these enticing destinations:

Luxor: The Open-Air Museum

Karnak Temple Complex: Step into the world's greatest ancient religious complex, where majestic temples, obelisks, and halls unfold the stories of pharaohs and gods.

Valley of the Kings: Explore the royal tombs, including the legendary tomb of Tutankhamun, in this necropolis on the west bank of the Nile.

Luxor Temple: A testimony to ancient Egyptian construction, this temple becomes magnificent when illuminated at night.

Hatshepsut's Temple: Marvel at the funerary temple dedicated to the mighty Queen Hatshepsut, set against the cliffs of Deir el-Bahari.

Hot Air Balloon Ride: Drift above the Valley of the Kings at sunrise for a stunning aerial perspective of Luxor's archaeological wonders.

Aswan: Nubian Beauty by the Nile Philae Temple: Delve into the mythological legends at this relocated temple dedicated to Isis, set on Agilkia Island.

High Dam: Witness modern engineering and enjoy panoramic views of Lake Nasser, a massive reservoir.

Nubian Village Excursion: Sail in a felucca to a Nubian village, experiencing the rich culture, bright colors, and friendly hospitality.

Unfinished Obelisk: Discover the huge obelisk abandoned in the granite quarries, revealing insights into ancient stone-carving processes.

Elephantine Island: Visit this ancient island with archaeological ruins and enjoy a calm respite from the hectic city.

Nile Cruises: Sailing Through History
Cruise Experience: Embark on a Nile cruise between Luxor and Aswan, admiring the magnificent scenery and stopping at significant sites along the way.

Kom Ombo Temple: Visit the double temple dedicated to Sobek and Horus, exhibiting a distinctive symmetrical design.

Edfu Temple: Explore one of the best-preserved temples in Egypt, dedicated to the falcon god Horus.

Nubian Museum (Aswan): Unearth the Nubian history and culture in this museum, showcasing items from the region.

Practical Tips: Best Time to Visit: Winter months (October to February) offer cooler temperatures for sightseeing.

Local Cuisine: Relish Nubian and Egyptian meals, with Aswan famed for its unique flavors.

Traditional Markets: Bargain for souvenirs in Aswan's markets, noted for Nubian crafts and spices.

Guided Tours: Engage qualified guides to understand the historical significance of each location.

Transportation: Domestic Flights: Connect to Luxor and Aswan via domestic flights from Cairo or other major cities.

rail Journey: Experience a magnificent rail trip along the Nile, linking Cairo to Luxor and Aswan.

Luxor and Aswan, with their historic charm and Nile's ageless flow, promise an immersing trip through the heart of Egypt's history. From colossal temples to calm river excursions, these places entice travelers to learn the secrets of an extraordinary culture.

Conclusion

10.1 Reflecting on Cairo's Endless Wonders

As your exploration of Cairo, the bustling centre of Egypt, comes to an end, take a minute to think on the various delights you've encountered. From historical marvels to modern joys, Cairo offers a tapestry of encounters that stay in the memory:

Ancient Echoes: Pyramids of Giza: Stand in wonder before the eternal pyramids, guardians of Egypt's ancient mysteries.

Sphinx's Gaze: Feel the enigmatic gaze of the Sphinx, a mute witness to centuries of history.

magnificent Mosques: Immerse yourself in the peacefulness of Islamic Cairo, where magnificent mosques weave a tapestry of spiritual beauty.

Coptic Heritage: Explore the hallowed sites of Coptic Cairo, where the roots of Christianity run deep.

Egyptian Museum Treasures: Wander through the halls of the Egyptian Museum, a treasure trove of antiques narrating tales of pharaohs and dynasties.

Modern Marvels: New Cairo's Architecture: Marvel at the contemporary architectural gems that embellish New Cairo, reflecting the city's vibrant personality.

Nile Corniche Serenity: Stroll along the Nile Corniche, where the river's leisurely flow matches the city's timeless cadence.

Culinary Delights: Indulge in the diverse flavors of Egyptian cuisine, from street food delights to luxury dining experiences.

Artistic Expressions: Navigate Cairo's modern art scene, where creativity blooms in galleries and urban places.

Endless Exploration: Cultural Diversity: Witness the peaceful blend of traditions and modernity, a monument to Cairo's unique cultural fabric.

Vibrant marketplaces: Lose yourself in the bustling marketplaces and bazaars, where the spirit of trade intertwines with everyday life.

Timeless Nile vistas: Whether from a felucca or the crowded bridges, admire the ever-changing vistas of the Nile.

Nightlife Extravaganza: Experience the colourful nightlife that fills Cairo's evenings with music, dance, and laughter.

Farewell, Cairo:

As you bid farewell to Cairo, let the echoes of its bustling streets, the aroma of its marketplaces, and the grandeur of its monuments linger in your heart. Whether you wanted historical wisdom, cultural immersion, or modern joys, Cairo has opened its treasures for you. Carry these experiences with you as you begin on your next voyage, enriched by the countless delights of this intriguing city. Ma'a as-salama, Cairo!

10.2 Future of Travel in Cairo

As Cairo continues to expand and adapt to the contemporary world, the future of tourism in this ancient city is poised to deliver even more engaging and convenient experiences for travellers. Here's what you can anticipate:

Technological Integration

Smart City Developments: New Cairo and other places are expected to integrate more smart technology, increasing navigation, information access, and environmental sustainability.

Digital Enhancements: Augmented reality (AR) and virtual reality (VR) experiences could bring ancient sites to life, giving rich historical tales straight on your smartphone or through customised tours.

Online Accessibility: Greater online access to services, from e-tickets for monuments and museums to digital maps and guides, will make it easier to organise and change itineraries on the go.

Sustainable and Responsible Tourism
Eco-Friendly Initiatives: Efforts to conserve Cairo's historical and natural ecosystems might include increased green spaces, pollution reduction measures, and sustainable tourism practices.

Community-Based Tourism: There could be an increase in experiences that directly benefit local communities, offering authentic cultural encounters while boosting local economies.

Infrastructure and Transportation Improvements
Public Transit Expansion: Continued expansion of Cairo's metro and bus networks, coupled with new bridges and

highways, aims to reduce congestion and provide accessibility to key tourist attractions.

Airport Modernization: Upgrades to Cairo International Airport and maybe new airports to accommodate the increased number of passengers, improving overall travel experience.

Diversifying Experiences Beyond the Beaten Path: Encouraging exploration of lesser-known locations in and around Cairo to distribute tourist impact and exhibit the city's hidden beauties.

Cultural Festivals and Events: An rise in cultural events, festivals, and exhibitions, both for international and domestic audiences, could promote greater cultural immersion and comprehension.

Health and Wellness Tourism: Growth in health-oriented travel offerings, including spa, wellness, and medical tourism, tapping into the global trend towards health-conscious vacations.

Enhanced Safety and Accessibility

Safety Measures: Strengthening safety measures, particularly in tourist-heavy regions, to offer a secure experience for tourists.

Accessibility Improvements: Efforts to make historical sites and city amenities more accessible to travelers with disabilities, including enhanced walkways, information access, and transportation.

Looking Ahead

The future of travel in Cairo is a blend of honoring its rich, historic past and embracing technology and sustainability. This transformation promises to make Cairo not simply a window into the past, but a dynamic, accessible, and stimulating destination for all kinds of travelers in the years to come.

Acknowledgements

In developing this thorough reference to Cairo, Egypt, a plethora of sources, travel specialists, and cultural authority have contributed to the construction of a rich and realistic representation of this great city. I convey my appreciation to the following:

Historical and Cultural Experts: Scholars and historians who have dedicated their knowledge to the understanding of Cairo's rich history, allowing for an in-depth exploration.

Tourism & Travel Agencies: The insightful insights supplied by travel agencies and tourism specialists have considerably contributed to the practical and current travel information in this guide.

Local Guides and Residents: Heartfelt gratitude to the locals, guides, and residents of Cairo who freely contributed their expertise, viewpoints, and passion for their city.

Government and Cultural Institutions: The help and information provided by government entities, cultural institutions, and tourism boards have been crucial in guaranteeing the accuracy of the content.

Photographers and Content Creators: The magnificent graphics accompanying the text are the result of the great photographers and content creators who have visually captured the spirit of Cairo.

Feedback from Users: Input from users who have explored past versions of this book has been invaluable, helping revise and enrich the content.

Cairo is a city that weaves together the threads of its ancient past and lively present, and it is my hope that this book serves as a helpful companion to those wishing to discover and appreciate the delights it has to offer.